Learn To Meditate

Learn To Meditate

THE JOURNEY TO SELF-DISCOVERY

S. G. McKeever

Printed in the United States of America

Editors: Mairi McKeever
Dhrirata Ferency
Terry Eldredge
Brian Moody

Interior Design: Jonathan Parker
Gochar K. Mursinna

Front Cover Artwork: Denis Caron

Back Cover Photo: Astika Mason

ISBN 1-885479-03-4

For additional information contact:
McKeever Publishing
P.O. Box 161167
San Diego, California 92176

San Diego • San Francisco • Fairfax

Contents

A BREATH FROM ETERNITY

It is now when the silence is sweet,
In the hours
Between night and day,
When words spring forth
From some eternal well,
Through this mind
Into these hands,
And onto eternity's page

Yet, who is the author?
Whose name shall I sign
When all has been written and said?
And people await the moment
To know from where
All this came,
And my hand shakes
As it does not know,
Nor my pen, nor mind,
Nor thoughts that seek
To trace their source.
Few can remember
The breath that gave
Them life.

Section I

The Foundations of Meditation

THE HEART OF MAN

Breaking away from fear and sorrow
Reaching out, alone, for tomorrow.
Knowing there are people behind, ahead
Yet travelling on
A dusty road, forging
To keep pace with a thousand dreams
Acting, yet fearing not the results
A compelling belief in Self
That stretches ever forward
Urges me on
Into the heart of man.

1

Introduction

Meditation is a practice which has developed over many thousands of years. Meditation has played, and continues to play, an important role in the cultivation of spiritual energies in the lives of many individuals and nations. Through the practice of meditation we awaken to the spirit which is the essence of our being.

This book has been created to provide you with safe and simple techniques for learning and experiencing concentration, relaxation and meditation. I will also present a solid basis of information so that you will understand the 'how and why' of the art of meditation which begins in learning concentration and focusing exercises.

The intensity, energy and commitment required for such an undertaking is tremendous, as are the powers and forces which are accessed and unleashed during the meditation process. The dormant potential within each of us is both unimaginable and, all too often, unexplored.

Ideally, due to the immensity of this journey of discovery, meditation should be studied and practiced under the guidance of a genuine spiritual teacher. A true spiritual teacher can oversee our spiritual growth, steering us clear of potential pitfalls and guiding us towards the supreme goal of existence–the awareness and embodiment of the fount of existence. It is said that when a student is ready, the teacher appears.

A walk on the beach, a hike through the woods, listening and relaxing to the sounds of nature, gardening, helping others, exercising, writing, painting, creating: all of these activities prepare us for experiencing meditation.

Meditation is communion with the source of life. Many of us have lost or never even felt this connection. In reconnecting with our source, we become conscious of the miracle of life, happening every moment within and around us.

Our conscious effort towards this awareness of our deepest depths is meditation. Theories and ideas cannot replace experience. Touching our source requires patience, practice and determination. Our persistent effort will assuredly bring the results we seek: doubt will be replaced by confidence, questions by knowledge and thought by action. These changes require of us an invitation to newness and the courage to let go of all that which binds and limits our consciousness.

Throughout this book there are exercises designed to aid you in learning how to focus, relax and meditate. To experience meditation you must do more than read. Try all of the exercises as they appear during your reading. Note which ones work best for you and from those which you prefer, create your own daily meditation program. Developing a daily meditation practice is the effort necessary to experience deeper and higher realms of being and awareness. Meditation, as with anything, is learned by regular practice; that is why there are specific exercises for you to do while reading. These exercises are the essence of this work. Please do them.

2

Words

Meditation opens us to a realm of experience which is difficult and challenging to express through words. Meditation is an experience. Through words we can effectively convey thoughts and ideas, yet it is difficult to convey experience. We can offer a description or approximation of the experience, yet rarely the experience itself. When writing or speaking on meditation the challenge is in expressing and conveying the actual experience.

Different words mean different things to different people. Connotation and individual experience often alter the definition of a word, thereby removing the definition that was the original intent of the writer.

Some people feel confined by certain words because of their upbringing and the way various philosophies attach connotations to words.

As far as this writing is concerned, let us return to the innate meanings of words that fell from the lips of those who sought to express the inexpressible.

For the purpose of this writing, the word God will represent the entirety of existence. In an effort to discern and distinguish different aspects of reality, I will use words such as Truth, Peace, Light, Eternity and Soul to represent realms of existence and experience which are aspects of God's Infinitude.

Brahma is the Sanskrit word for God. In the following poem, Ralph Waldo Emerson, the American poet, philosopher and sage describes the omnipresence of God:

Brahma

If the red slayer think he slays,
Or if the slain think he is slain,
They know not well the subtle ways
I keep, and pass, and turn again.

Far or forgot to me is near;
Shadow and sunlight are the same;
The vanished gods to me appear;
And one to me are shame and fame.

They reckon ill who leave me out;
When me they fly, I am the wings;
I am the doubter and the doubt,
And I the hymn the Brahmin sings.

The strong gods pine for my abode,
And pine in vain the sacred Seven;
But thou, meek lover of the good!
Find me, and turn thy back on heaven.

God is not a concept, God is not a point of philosophical discussion. God is a reality. God is the highest, deepest, vastest reality that each one of us can conceive and imagine. Just as our consciousness evolves and expands, so can our awareness of God.

"The light that shines above the heavens and above this world, the light that shines in the highest world, beyond which there are no others–that is the light that shines in the hearts of men."

– Chandogya Upanishad

Our meditation-journey leads us into ever-transcending realms of awareness and consciousness. As our eyes steadily open to a vast inner landscape we discover realms of concentration, emotion, thought and reality that we cannot now even imagine. The experience which today we take as failure and defeat, tomorrow becomes a lesson in humility and the day after appears as an opportunity for inner growth. So too, as we become more conscious, our awareness and reality change. Today God may mean good fortune. Tomorrow we may experience God as Peace and Light. The day after tomorrow God may appear as Truth and Infinity, and finally, we may come to know God as an ever-expanding oneness of multiplicity and diversity.

God may appear to be masculine, feminine, formless, personified, changeless, ever-transcending, etc. In other words, God can take on infinite aspects depending on the consciousness of the observer. In meditation we reach for, and grow into, God.

An awareness of our own growing, changing conception and awareness of God will give us tolerance and understanding when interacting with the customs, beliefs and realisations of others.

EXERCISE 1

Take a few moments and see what image you associate with the word God. If the image which comes into your mind is not compelling to you, then create an image of God that makes you aspire to commune with God. Reread this chapter to familiarize yourself with the various aspects you can incorporate into your image of God.

3

Philosophy & Understanding

Theory and concept are created for conceptualization and understanding. Meditation, in its true form, is an entirely experiential process. The essence of meditation is in our practice and experience—what we do and how we feel. This book does not emphasize theory or philosophy. This book emphasizes experience and practice. Nevertheless, theory and philosophy can provide the necessary backdrop for us to mentally formulate and understand our practice of meditation. This mental understanding is helpful. Meditation is most fulfilling if seen as an all-encompassing action. Our progress in meditation comes not in rejection but in acceptance. Theory and concept provide a representation of reality which helps our mind grasp the meditation experience.

An understanding of basic Eastern philosophy is beneficial to the understanding of meditation. The underlying concept is that we each possess within ourselves a spark of the Infinite. As Christ said, "The Kingdom of Heaven is within." We find this same concept in Buddhism, Hinduism, Islam and Judaism. Meditation is the act of reconnecting with this Heaven, Spirit, Nirvana, Soul, *atman,* Infinite and Eternal within ourselves.

That which stands between ourselves and the Infinite is not the concept of right and wrong, good and bad, or an external judgment system, but rather a lack of awareness. This is attributed to our mind's inability to perceive Truth. In essence, the reason we are not conscious of our Immortality is because our own mind, our own awareness, is not able to grasp the Truth, even though that Truth exists within and around us at every moment. By approaching life through the Spirit we are able to rekindle the awareness of our deeper selves. Throughout history true spiritual teachers have said, and continue to tell seekers, "God-realization is our birthright." Every man, every woman, all humankind is born with that essence, that spark of Spirit. Imagine a great fire blazing, the fire of creation. Candles sweep by, and as they move over the fire each wick is lit–a separate flame is created on each individual candle. These separate flames represent our individuality, our uniqueness. The fire from which we have all been created is God.

We often think of ourselves as complex beings with many parts. Just as we can see a tree as a single entity, so too we can see each individual as one entity. Yet, as we begin to dissect a tree with our minds and senses, we find many parts: leaves, branches, a root system and a trunk. In a human being, we find a body, breath, emotion, mind, desire, thought, memory, a soul and many other aspects. The concept of what a human being actually is differs according to various cultures and philosophies. I find it helpful to look at people as consisting of five primary aspects.

First is the physical body, of which we are all well aware. Our body is comprised of our muscles, cells, bones, blood, tissue, and so on.

Next we have our emotional energy, which is called our vital: the energy within our bodies that seeks to sustain and increase life and our connection with the earth. The vital energy can be felt primarily in the three lower *chakras* or energy centers (see chapter 6), beginning at the base of the spine and extending into the region of the solar plexus.

The third aspect of being is our mind: the thought process. Everyone reading this book knows how to think and use his or her mind. As we seek to understand ourselves and all that surrounds us we refine and make more exact and perfect our thinking. Through this refinement we have reached great heights of awareness and understanding. We find examples of this awareness in Socrates, Plato, Spinoza, St. Augustine, Einstein and a myriad of other great thinkers who have been expanding the known world through their own probing minds.

There are limits to our mind's capacity to grasp and assimilate knowledge and wisdom. The limits are defined by our senses, which supply the mind with the majority of the information upon which it functions. The mind may create and operate technology, yet not consider the consequences. Thoughts, though often productive, can also be counterproductive: self-doubt, jealousy, anxiety, nervousness, and worry are all products of our mind.

The next aspect of ourselves, of which some are aware, is the heart—the spiritual heart. The spiritual heart is located in the center of the chest, at the point where you would gesture when referring to how you sincerely feel about something. This is not our physical heart, but our spiritual heart. The spiritual heart is said to be the seat of love, oneness and compassion.

Feeling compassion for all beings plays an essential role in Buddhism. An example of heart-centered oneness would be the work of Mother Teresa. Her work is not based on her mind's desire to acquire, her mind's desire for fame or profit, but rather on the heart-centered feeling of oneness. When we see suffering and injustice in the world we are often drawn to action by our feeling of oneness. This is not a feeling that we have to create; it is a reality within us. Just as we do not have to create our physical body or imagine our physical body for it to exist, so too we do not have to mentally fabricate oneness—it is within us at all times.

The last aspect of our being is the soul, or the Infinite, the Eternal, the Immortal within us, the spark of the divine. The soul is the oneness each of us has with God. The goal of meditation is to become conscious of our soul.

"God-realization" is a term used in Eastern philosophy to describe the achievement of one who has become conscious of his or her eternal, infinite aspect. Another term used to describe this state of awareness is "self-realization": realizing one's true self. These terms are interchangeable.

One of the pitfalls of modern thinking, which stems from the power technology has created, is to view ourselves mechanically, to see ourselves as machines. I prefer conceptualizing people as primarily spiritual beings: spirit existing in matter. This awareness of spirit links all existence in an interlocking holistic reality—interrelating all of existence; not just physically, but emotionally, mentally, psychically, and spiritually. In our practice of meditation, it is counterproductive to think of ourselves as machines, to think of our minds as machines, to think that every meditation experience will be the same, or to think of progress as some theoretical ascending scale. It is not. In an organic system things are constantly changing. The world and all within it is in a constant state of flux. Life is not linear, although we attempt to perceive it as such. There is a cyclical and interconnected aspect to life that will become apparent through meditation.

The experience of discovering our true nature–the journey we undertake each time we meditate–necessitates a constant flexibility in our theories and conceptualizations regarding ourselves and all of life. Through meditation we experience deep emotions such as sincerity, gratitude, love and purity which, once experienced, radically alter our view of ourselves and our potential. Each time we discover something new about ourselves we discover something new about existence, about the world around us. The same forces which drive our very atoms and molecules drive the heavenly bodies through space. By becoming aware of our energy source–the source which keeps our heart beating–we become aware of the force which whirls the earth around the sun.

Concepts and philosophy emerge out of experience, and therefore, as our experiences change, so shall our concepts. Most people cling to one concept–afraid of the ever-new realm of experience. The individual who meditates has the courage to let go of the thought/concept realm and plunge into the realm of direct experience.

The ideas that have been presented so far are intended to provide a framework through which to understand your own experiences. Through meditation one can see the truth-essence in all philosophies and religions. Meditation is pure spirituality. Spirituality is the road, the common road, that all people share. Religion is the individual's house. Within that house there are customs, traditions, and structures with which each of us feels comfortable. But in the morning, as people leave their homes to go to town, they share a common road. This is the road of spirituality. That is the road this book will help you to discover. An ancient proverb states, "Paths are many, Truth is one." To seek oneness in diversity is an age-old challenge for humankind.

Theories and ideas help us to function on the mental level. Meditation leads us to a level of awareness where thought and concept give way to experience. Once we attain this deeper awareness we can look back and see the truth-essence in different ideas and at the same time possess the experience of underlying unity of existence which is an awareness far transcending mental concepts.

4

Meditation: A Step Towards God

Yoga is a Sanskrit word meaning union. Through the practice of *yoga* we seek to unify our existence and awareness with God. Meditation, *dyana* in Sanskrit, is one aspect of this effort. It is generally taught that there are eight stages, or steps, in *yoga*. By reviewing these we can better understand the place and significance of meditation.

Yama means control and signifies the seeker's acceptance of, and adherence to, the basic moral commandments. These are universal: non-violence, truthfulness, non-stealing, continence and non-covetousness. Continence, in thought, word and deed is necessary if one is to transcend all sense impressions, master the thought process and merge into pure spirit. Continence is, of course, possible only at certain stages of a person's life, yet it has been put forward by genuine spiritual teachers as a necessary step towards total liberation.

Niyama involves the cultivation of virtues. This is the next step in the process of *yoga* whereby we actively change and mold our character towards a higher ideal. The virtues include simplicity, sincerity, purity, contentment and wisdom. The last of these is attained through the study of the sacred scriptures which form the basis of humankind's religions.

Asana is a term which denotes a physical stance or posture. *Asanas* are most familiar in the West as the postures of *hatha yoga.* Here the seeker attempts to bring steadiness, strength and stillness to the very essence of our earth-existence: the body and nervous system. This is achieved through the practice of various postures and movements.

Pranayama means the control of life-force. *Pranayama* should not be attempted until one has developed the necessary strength and discipline through the various *asanas.* In *pranayama* the process of breathing is slowed, controlled and altered in order to develop a calm and steady mind and the willpower that comes through discipline. Mind and breath are linked. By controlling breath we control mind.

Pratyahara is the first step in the practice often thought of as meditation. This involves bringing the mind and senses under control. We then direct our perceptions inward towards God. This is the great moment when the seeker turns from absorption in the outer world and begins to become aware of the inner world which is beyond form, time and space.

Dharana is the seeker's effort to gather up all of the latent powers of mind through the practice of concentration. By disciplining the mind to focus on a single point we bring the power and force of concentration into our consciousness. By anchoring our mind upon a single point we create a deep stillness in our awareness. This focus opens the door to meditation.

Dhyana is meditation proper. True meditation is the result of long periods of concentration. Meditation is the experience of the potential awareness which lies beyond the realm of mind. Meditation is experienced in two primary forms. The first is when the object of concentration is let go and the mind expands limitlessly. The second is when the force of concentration is applied to the awakening of the spiritual heart wherein exists our conscious oneness with all of creation and the unity of the individual soul with the universal soul.

Samadhi is traditionally considered the goal of *yoga*. *Samadhi* is the attainment of infinite peace. The Buddhist term for *samadhi* is *nirvana*. The Christian would term *samadhi* the "Heaven within." *Samadhi* is attained through long periods of meditation.

The attainment of *samadhi* traditionally marked the end of the seeker's journey. Released from the duality, pain and suffering of earthly life the seeker sought eternal release in the bliss of *samadhi*. This retreat from life is not the only possibility. There are various degrees of *samadhi*–the highest being *sahaja samadhi*. Here the seeker brings the bliss of infinite peace into the earth arena through a continuation and acceptance of life. The ultimate aim being a transformation of, and not retreat from, the finite, fleeting world.

5

Prana, The Life-Force

To achieve a complete understanding of the forces at work in our existence let us begin with the primary life-force of the universe–*prana*. *Prana* is the great vital energy breathing and circulating through all of existence. Breathing, the most basic and fundamental function of the living organism, involves the intake and regulation of *prana*. *Prana* is the life-force of the nervous system upon which we depend for existence. Once we become aware of the power of *prana* and the significance of each breath we take, we gain an immediate insight into the underlying principles upon which various Eastern disciplines are based. These include the martial arts, Chinese medicine, Indian medicine, *Hatha Yoga* (a branch of *yoga* which seeks to gain illumination beginning with a perfection of the body through various physical poses, or *asanas*), breath control–*pranayama* (*prana* = life-force, *yama* = control). These and other practices stress an awareness of *prana* and control of life-force, via breathing. Without this life-force coursing through our system we will quickly die. All that we do–move, think, feel–is dependant upon *prana*.

The life-breath, *prana*, when thought of as sustaining life in the human body, is classified into five main categories according to the various functions performed by the energy. Later in this chapter we will discover that a few of these categories of function are related to specific *chakras*, or energy centers, in the body (see chapter 6).

The five categories into which life-force is classified are: *apana*, which moves in the region of the lower abdomen and trunk and presides over the lower functions; *samana*, which maintains the equilibrium of the vital forces and stokes the gastric fire and digestion; *vyana*, which distributes the vital energies derived from food and breath throughout the entire body; *prana* (here the word is used to note a particular aspect) which dwells in the upper part of the body and controls the heart and respiration, in effect, bringing the universal force into the physical system; and finally *udana*, which moves upward from the body to the crown of the head and controls the intake of food as well as channels the communication between the physical life and the greater life of the spirit.

There are three principle channels, or *nadis*, through which the life energy flows throughout the human organism. These channels are *ida*, *pingala* and *sushumna*. *Ida* carries *prana* from the left nostril through the left side of the body and down to the base of the spine. *Pingala* carries *prana* from the right nostril through the right side of the body and down to the base of the spine. *Ida* is the *nadi* of the moon and Mercury and is felt in mildness, calmness and coolness; *pingala* is the *nadi* of the sun and Mars and is felt in power and heat. Our "health"–both emotional and physical–is based upon the balancing of these different aspects of our being: masculine-feminine, yin-yang, power-calm, heat-cool. This essential balance can be maintained and regulated through a constant awareness of our breathing patterns and their regulation when necessary. This practice is known by the Sanskrit word *pranayama*.

The third *nadi* is *sushumna* which carries life-energy through the middle of the spinal column.

This channel is known to science as the vertebral canal. This is the main energy channel of the human being. It receives a ceaseless flow of life energy through which our existence is maintained, much as a vast body of water maintains the boat. When we are in deep sleep on a boat we are not aware of the water, yet it sustains our existence. So too, through the *sushumna nadi* our existence is maintained although we are only faintly aware of the energy coursing through every cell of our bodies.

Ida, Pingala and *Sushumna* intersect each other at various places called *chakras.* Each of these energy centers is formed like a disc or wheel. The name, location, color, seed-sound and qualities associated with each of these *chakras* are discussed at the end of this chapter.

Throughout history men and women have unveiled and discovered various and different routes to a oneness with God. One of these is *Kundhalini Yoga,* which involves the regulation and control over the *prana* flowing through the body. According to this practice the *Kundhalini,* or cosmic force, is sleeping dormant in the root *chakra.* Through *pranayama* this energy is aroused and made to go up the spinal column, awakening the energy centers. Realization, or illumination, comes when the crown *chakra* is awakened and the individual consciousness unites with God. *Kundhalini Yoga* is the most dangerous of all the *yogas* because the forces being regulated and aroused are essential to the proper functioning of the body. Any mishap will bear immediate physical, mental and emotional consequences.

The regulation of breathing which occurs naturally is an excellent way to regulate *prana* and bring vigor and balance to our system. These include times of deep, relaxed breathing such as the regulation of our breathing during and after exercise and developing a keen awareness of our breathing. Physical exercise brings peace, calmness and a natural balance to our system. Any further regulation of *prana* should only be done under the careful guidance of a knowledgeable *yoga* teacher.

Contrary to what is often taught in *Kundhalini Yoga*, it is not necessary to open the *chakras* in order to realise God. God can be realised through many paths, or types of *yoga*. The opening of the energy centers is only one method. Furthermore, the *chakras* do not necessarily need to be opened from the lowest to the highest. In fact, many modern spiritual teachers highly recommend first opening the heart center, located in the center of the chest.

Purity, unity, compassion, love and oneness are qualities which form the foundation for a balanced, healthy spiritual life. These attributes can be found in the awakening of the heart center. With the purity of our heart, we can explore realms of consciousness far beyond our imagination. Rather than focusing directly on the other *chakras*, I suggest plenty of exercise, a disciplined emotional life, community or selfless service, daily meditation and the pursuit of your creative interests. These activities will purify and awaken your energy centers in a safe and timely fashion.

EXERCISE 2

Take a few moments and write on a piece of paper each of these categories: Exercise, Self-giving and Creativity. Now write down some activities you can do which will allow you to focus your energy into these positive channels. Try to do at least one activity from each of these categoreis each day. By simply spending 5 to 10 minutes in each activity you are learning to channel your energy into spiritual and meditative pursuits. Remember, great journeys begin with one step.

6

The Chakras

The awakening of the *chakras* is achieved primarily through concentration, meditation and the help and guidance of a genuine teacher. Forms of concentration include visualization, the repetition of *mantras*, which are the 'seed-sounds' of physical, psychic and spiritual realities. By manifesting a seed-sound we begin to bring a particular reality into existence. By chanting or singing the seed-sound of a particular *chakra* we give resonance and strength to that potential energy within ourselves.

The *chakras* can also be awakened by focusing on and strengthening the qualities or attributes connected with the various energy centers. For example, to open the heart center you could chant the *mantra* YAM and cultivate the qualities of love, compassion and unity with all beings. As mentioned earlier, the *chakras* can also be opened by *pranayama* and *kundhalini yoga*.

The *chakras* are most often described as resembling the shape of multi-petaled, variously colored lotus flowers or rapidly spinning disks with a discernable number of spokes and colors.

In an effort to aid you in understanding these energy centers I have compiled the following information for each of the seven *chakras*: the Sanskrit name, the English name, physical location, number of petals, colors, the mantra used to awaken the *chakra*, the physical sense (taste, touch, sight, sound, smell) connected with the *chakra* and the qualities connected with the *chakra*. In addition, I will list the aspect of *prana* (the five aspects are listed at the beginning of the chapter on *prana*) or vital breath, associated with the *chakra* and the animal depicted as being identified with the particualr energy center. The animal embodies the qualities of the *chakra* as exemplified in the animal kingdom.

And now for the *chakras*:

Muladhara, the root *chakra*, is situated at the lower end of the spinal column in the pelvic region. It has four petals. The predominant colors are orange and red and the *mantra* for awakening this *chakra* is LAM. The sense of smell is connected with this *chakra*, the element is earth and the animal is a black elephant. The vital breath *apana* is connected with this center.

It is within the depths of this root *chakra* that the *kundhalini* energy lies dormant. This energy is feminine in nature and is the creative life-force of nature–symbolized by a snake laying dormant, coiled three and one-half times around the spine.

The root *chakra* has the qualities of solidity (as in the solid mass of earth upon which we exist and build) and resistance. An individual with access to this center can conquer disease and know or discover anything.

Svadhisthana, the spleen *chakra*, is situated in the region above the genitals, has six petals of which the color is blood red. The *mantra* for awakening this *chakra* is VAM. The sense of taste is connected with this *chakra*, the element is water and the ruling animal is the makara, a sea monster similar to a crocodile. The vital breath is *samana*.

This *chakra* regulates the ocean of fluids in the human body and constitutes the essence of the individual's personality. One with mastery over this center acquires the power of love: the ability to love and be loved by all of creation.

Manipura, the navel *chakra*, is situated in the solar plexus and has ten petals of which green is the predominant color. The seed-sound for awakening this *chakra* is RAM. The sense of sight, the element of fire and the animal ram are related to his center. The vital breath is *samana*.

It is said that concentration upon this center, sometimes referred to as the "abdominal brain," leads to a knowledge of the physical organism and its functions. One with mastery over this center conquers sorrow and suffering, gains healing power and attains access to realms of consciousness associated with the "underworld," or that realm into which we transition at death. It is interesting to note that the water of tears–both of sorrow and joy–restores balance to this fire center.

Anahata, the heart center, is situated in the region of the physical heart but it is aligned in the center of the chest and has twelve petals of a bright golden color. The sense of touch, the element air and the antelope are related to this center. The antelope, the vehicle for the Vedic God ofWinds, is noted for its swiftness and lightness of physical substance. The *mantra* here is YAM. The vital breath is *prana*.

The heart center is related to perpetual motion and is said to be the seat of the individual soul. An individual with mastery over this center experiences the bliss of oneness with all of existence and is able to merge into the vastness of life. In the heart one transcends time and space and can travel anywhere in the subtle body.

Vishuddha, the throat center, is situated at the juncture of the spinal column and medula oblongata, or more generally at the base of the throat and is related to the thyroid. *Vishuddha* has sixteen petals of a blue-green color. The senses of sound and hearing, the element of ether and the moon-white elephant are related to this center. The seed-sound is HAM. The vital breath is *udana.*

This is a pure and mild center in that it poses no dangers upon being opened whereas the other centers–except the heart–can awaken powers which we may be tempted to misuse for selfish purposes rather than for the fulfilment of God's Will. One with mastery over this center developes the capacity to offer divine messages to the world through music, art, literature and other mediums. With the insight from this center one discovers the underlying principles of the universe and can retain eternal youth–but, as Sri Aurobindo questioned, "Who would want to wear the same jacket for one hundred years?"

Ajna, the brow center or third eye, is located just below the center of the forehead. *Ajna* has two primary petals of rose color each with 48 smaller petals making a total of 96. The sense here is mind–the lord and overseer of the other senses, the element is undifferentiated energy, the level of energy before it descends into the realm of duality and the play of opposites. The seed-sound is AUM.

It is upon the opening of this center that the unity of existence is established and the seeker passes beyond the realm of duality. If we think of God, or undifferentiated consciousness, descending into creation we can say that it is here in the third eye that duality begins to manifest. The duality necessary for creation–yin and yang–is represented by the two petals of this *chakra*–representing the play of opposites necessary for the manifestation of life. The two petals also represent the two hemispheres of the brain, the perfect balance of which developes the sixth sense–intuition. The 96 smaller petals inside the two petals represent the multiplicity of creation.

The individual with mastery over this center achieves psychic and occult powers that defy all limits. The third-eye has the power that God is. This is the most powerful center–it is the meeting place of *Ida*, *Pingala* and *Sushumna*.

Sahasrara, the crown center, is said to manifest five finger widths above the crown of the head. It is also associated with the pineal gland. The pineal gland lies near the center of the brain and is believed by Western science to play a key role in human sexuality and regulating the body's daily and seasonal adaptation to changing levels of light. Besides these apparent functions the other functions of the gland are unknown to Western science. *Sahasrara* is a lotus of 972 petals of which the predominant color is violet.

This center is an amalgamation of all the lower centers. This is the culmination of our aspirations for peace, spirit, delight and God. The awakening of the crown *chakra* brings infinite bliss and an inseparable oneness with God. At this center of quintessential consciousness, the transcendental–the ever-transcending aspect of existence–is experienced as one passes beyond the boundaries of time and space.

All of the *chakras* are linked to one another via the nervous system and the psychic channels in the body. Because of these links we are able to purify and strengthen the lower three *chakras* by our concentration and efforts to awaken the heart center, throat *chakra*, third eye and crown *chakra*.

By focusing on love, compassion, purity, creativity, enthusiasm and wisdom, we will awaken and purify our entire being. Attempting to open the lower *chakras* without these qualities can prove disastrous. The force of the universe pulses through our bodies. Awakening the powers of the *chakras* without the knowledge to control them is like handing a sharp knife to a young child. First focus on the heart center or throat *chakra.* In order to open these you will need to cultivate a focused, pure and dynamic consciousness. In the process of learning to bring forward this energy in your life you will naturally transform and purify your lower *chakras.*

To unite this view of the *chakras* with our earlier framework we will say that the lower three *chakras*–the root, spleen and navel–comprise our vital energy, the lower two being the lower vital and the solar plexus our higher vital.

The heart center and third eye *chakra* are integrally linked and can be seen as slightly different manifestations of the same energy. We can view them as husband and wife–complimentary aspects of a wholeness. We can view the third eye as power and illumination and the heart as sweetness and love–hence the heart is feminine, the third eye masculine.

The soul or psychic being is the crown *chakra,* an amalgamation or result of the purification, perfection and transformation of the human consciousness.

Modern science most often identifies the brain as the seat of consciousness while the other organs, glands and body parts as being machine-like and not connected with awareness and intelligence. In contrast, the ideas I have presented regarding the *chakras* and the corresponding organs and glands connected with them present a view wherein consciousness resides throughout the entire body. This latter view has been the essence of Chinese and Indian medicine for thousands of years and has just recently begun to be acknowledged by Western scientists.

The brain's communication network is created by billions of brain cells, called neurons. Information travels between neurons via chemical reactions and the transfer of electrochemical energy. Modern science has identified neuropeptides as a vital component in the brain's communication network. These neuropeptides are key elements in the triggering of emotions. Scientifically, emotion could be defined as neuropeptides stimulating electrochemical changes in the brain.

Scientists have discovered that neuropeptides are produced not only in the brain but also in the dorsal horn or coccyx of the spine (root *chakra*); spleen (spleen *chakra*); thymus (throat *chakra*); lymph glands (the largest of which is in the region of the navel *chakra*) and heart (heart center). Hence, our emotions and awareness are created by the entire body, especially those areas where the '*chakras*' exist.

Although these and other "discoveries" regarding the integral connection between body and mind are new to Western science, they have been known to Chinese and Indian doctors for thousand of years. Chinese medicine stresses the necessity of maintaining a balanced energy flow throughout the entire body. The liver, heart, kidneys, spleen and lungs are emphasized as key elements in the flow of life-force and consciousness throughout the body. These organs communicate, according to Chinese medicine, via meridians or energy channels. This knowledge forms the foundation for acupuncture which corrects imbalances along these lines of communication.

An awareness of our bodies and the spectacular currents of energy coursing within and around us is a great step towards an awareness of God. By understanding ourselves we begin to understand the vastness of existence.

By focusing on the *chakras* we begin to become aware of these energies. We begin this journey with symbols, sounds, visualizations and the knowledge set forth by others. With patience and persistence we begin to experience directly these energies.

I want to once again reiterate that our practice of meditation should begin with the heart center. The heart center is the seat of love, oneness and compassion. As we expand our awareness and become conscious of our abilities and powers it is essential that we have access to the wisdom that emerges from the heart center. The wisdom of oneness and compassion will guide us safely to our destination.

7

The Yogas & Meditation

Hatha Yoga

Yoga is a Sanskrit word meaning "union with God." The type of *yoga* we are most familiar with in the West is undoubtedly *Hatha Yoga*: '*Ha*' is Sanskrit for sun and '*tha*' is moon. *Hatha* therefore is the bringing together of all existence into a wholeness and unity. *Hatha yoga* begins with physical postures designed to strengthen the physical body and nervous system. The spine is strengthened and all internal organs and functions are enhanced.

Once these postures, or '*asanas*,' are mastered (and this can easily require years of daily, regular practice), we begin the practice of *pranayama. Pranayama* is the practice of regulating one's breathing. The mind is affected by our breathing and our breathing is affected by our mind. When we are fearful or nervous we take shallow, short breaths. When we are calm and relaxed, we breathe deeply and fully. By recognizing this interconnection we can devise ways to make our minds calm and peaceful by slowing down our breathing patterns. This is the essence of *pranayama.* The breathing process is lengthened and slowed by a conscious filling of the lungs as fully as possible. This involves a conscious contraction of the stomach muscles, a lengthening of the spine and diaphram, and a determined effort to opening the lungs to as much air as possible which involves the muscles of the ribs, shoulders and spine.

Once *pranayama* is mastered (and this, it is said, should never even be attempted without the guidance of a genuine spiritual master) the seeker has gained immense awareness of the wonderous powers within the human frame. The seeker comes to know the universe by knowing the individual's universe: the body. The same force which guides the galaxies courses through the human frame. As we breathe in we can feel all of existence coursing through our veins.

It is now that the seeker awakens the potentiality of existence, consciousness and delight-bliss lying in unmanifested seed form in the base of the spine. This energy embodies creation, preservation and transformation and is the essence of all. As this energy rises through the spinal column the psychic energy centers awaken and the human being awakens from finite consciousness into infinite consciousness.

There are other paths of *yoga* that lead to the same result though through different means. All *yogas* must present a means whereby the mind is transformed from its current level of awareness and made fit to provide a channel whereby the human consciousness can receive purer and more unified perceptions. In *Hatha yoga* the mind is stilled by regulating the physical organism.

Raja Yoga

Raja Yoga begins with the practice of stilling the body and mind through concentration of the mind on a single thought or sensory experience, i.e. sight, sound, scent, touch or taste. Through this concentration the mind becomes stilled to a single point. As your ability to concentrate expands you can then concentrate on the very building blocks of creation. Ultimately, to attain liberation, you must focus first on your image of God and then on God as beyond image and form. Concentration and meditation form the essence of *Raja Yoga*.

Jnana Yoga

Jnana Yoga is the *yoga* of knowledge and discrimination. Relative existence arises from the forces of intelligence and power. By seeking pure and correct knowledge we align ourselves with one of the building blocks of existence.

Discrimination is the mind's greatest power. As human beings we are capable of discriminating between that which is eternal and everlasting and that which is fleeting and transitory. The seeker of God must learn to discriminate between the soul, which is immortal and eternal, and those things which are in a state of flux. Through discrimination we find and experience the substratum of all existence: God. The path of knowledge also entails recognizing This substratum in all transient forms we encounter. The wise woman sees God within her children and husband. The unwise man worships money and property as his god. Jesus' words resonate the wisdom of true discrimination: "For how would a man be benefitted, if he should gain the whole world and lose his own soul." (Matthew 16:26)

Bhakti Yoga

Bhakti *Yoga* is the *yoga* of devotion and higher emotions. This *yoga* has three steps–love, devotion and surrender. First we learn to love God; then we devote ourselves to God's Will trying, as best we can, to live our lives in service to God.

Finally, we surrender our finite existence into the very breath of God. This surrender is our realization of the oneness between God and man. In *Bhakti Yoga* we cultivate these emotions and transform our worldly emotions into divine emotions. This is achieved through the cultivation of sincerity, simplicity, purity and gratitude. These feelings prepare the soil of our existence so that we may grow, from our very human roots, the God-becoming tree with its three vast branches: love, devotion and surrender.

One of the greatest challenges in *Bhakti Yoga* is cultivating a love for God. It is difficult to love that which we cannot perceive. It is here that the *guru*, or genuine spiritual teacher, plays a key role. The *guru* has merged his or her consciousness with God and therefore God can manifest Himself or Herself to the seekers in and through the *guru*. The disciple experiences God through interaction with the *guru*. We can surely feel and sense God in various ways, yet to see God reflected in human form is undoubtedly the representation with which human beings will most identify.

Karma Yoga

Karma Yoga is selfless service. We all know what selfishness is: immersion of oneself in one's own ego and self-gratification. Selflessness is the conscious giving up of one's self-importance so as to experience the joy of one's release into the infinity of all of existence. This process is intensified by acting for the betterment of the lives of others. This type of *yoga* is exemplified in the tradition of feeding the hungry, nursing the aged, clothing the poor and sheltering all in need. This giving is not limited towards helping those in pain or need. Self-giving can embody the offering of our creativity, wisdom, knowledge, love, gratitude and feeling of unity to humanity. This can be done through art, teaching, community work and selfless meditation. Selfless meditation is an intense, deep state of awareness wherein we thrust our very life breath into humanity for we have come to realise the infinite delight of true self-giving. In *Karma yoga* we serve God in all.

Karma yoga challenges the seeker by demanding constant observance of oneself to ensure that action does not become selfish. In this way the "I" gives way to "oneness."

Kundhalini Yoga

In the earlier chapter: *Prana, the Life-Force*, I explained the principles underlying the practice of *Kundhalini Yoga. Kundhalini Yoga* focuses on the awakening of the *chakras* in ascending order beginning with *muladhara*, the root chakra. This process begins with the practice of *pranayama* whereby the seeker becomes aware of, and ultimately learns to control, the flow of *prana* throughout the body.

Once *prana* is adequately controlled the seeker then awakens the *kundhalini* energy which lies dormant in the root *chakra* in the base of the spine. The seeker directs the rising of this energy through the energy channels. As the energy rises the *chakras* awaken. With the opening of *sahasrara*, the crown *chakra*, the consciousness of the individual merges with the infinite.

This is the most dangerous of all *yogas* because we are siezing control of, and altering, the body's life-force and we are awakening the lower *chakras*, the powers of which sway most seekers from the ultimate goal of meditation. For these reasons I highly recommend focusing on and awakening the heart center first. This center provides the wisdom, purity and love necessary for the understanding and use of the powers which arise with the opening of the lower *chakras*.

A genuine teacher is absolutely essential to oversee the control of life-force. A mistake or error in judgement can result in serious illness or even death. The powers of existence are not to be taken lightly or misused.

Integral Yoga

It is important to remember that meditation and our search for God need not be separate from our daily life. The idea of integrating all aspects of our life and being into our pursuit and acceptance of the infinite is one of the most profound ideas of the 20th century. Spirituality is not for the select few. It is for all.

In the past, spiritual life was considered to be a life of renunciation and austerity in which we were instructed to turn away from worldly pursuits and activities, enclosing ourselves in isolation in an effort to find God, truth and happiness. Integral *yoga* is acceptance. Rather than recoil from the world in order to find truth, we realise that this earthly life, in all its multiplicity and infinite variety, is our moment, our chance, for humanity's transformation into the divine and infinite. Only through acceptance can transformation take place. Through rejection and renunciation we deny life the opportunity to flower. This renunciation allows us a static peace yet only through acceptance can we experience the dynamic peace of ever-expanding existence and love.

Integral *yoga* gives inner significance to all aspects of life: keeping the body fit and healthy; eating well; taking regular exercise; reading inspiring spiritual writings; practicing meditation and self-giving; and serving our families, communities and world. The idea of integral *yoga* is to bring the balance and harmony accessed through meditation into all aspects of life.

Creativity, as an expression of our awareness of the inifinite descending into our lives, is another important aspect of integral *yoga*. This includes writing, playing music, singing, drawing, painting, athletics, *yoga* and many other activities. This creativity and conscious activity are not a proclamation of our greatness to the world or a result of our desire for name and fame. Rather, the creative expression is offered as a manifestation of the divinity within us. The beauty of the creative process is that we can offer to the world an expression of ourselves that is not bound by the dictates of the rules and regulations of society and the past. Often feelings, emotions and ideas cannot be expressed in words or predetermined mediums. Creativity offers us the freedom to create new channels through which to express ourselves.

Through the concept of Integral *Yoga* we can see the possibility for spiritual growth and understanding in all of our daily activities. The potential for an awareness of God's Presence within us exists in every moment. By being conscious and present in all of our activities we learn to attune our awareness towards our source. This is Integral *Yoga*.

Tantra Yoga

Tantra Yoga embraces the entirety of life–infinite and eternal–much like Integral *Yoga*. The *Tantric yogi* seeks God in the bliss of unmanifest potential and in the multiplicity and diversity of creation. *Tantra* is the ancient *yoga* from which Integral *Yoga* has taken shape.

To gain a complete understanding of *Tantra Yoga* we need to begin, as it were, at the beginning, which is, of course, with God. God has two distinct aspects, which can be termed silence and sound; passive and active; male and female; or, to use the *Sanskrit* terminology–*Purusha* and *Prakriti*.

The masculine reality of God is conceived as a silent, still, omniscient aspect. The feminine aspect is active, earthly and most visible in creation as nature. Most yogic systems place primary importance on the attainment of the static *Purusha* consciousness. This is achieved most rapidly by renouncing earthly life and interaction and escaping into the stillness of the static consciousness of God. In an effort to secure this realization, earthly attachments are shunned, renounced and seen as pitfalls on the road to enlightenment. For the philosophic justification of this method, the earth plane is characterized as an illusion which needs to be shunned in pursuit of God. Undeniably, this framework of understanding has been used successfully by hundreds of human beings to attain a unity with God, yet this method has not allowed for the transformation of human consciousness. Rejection of human consciousness for the divine–yes, transformation–no.

The transformation of human consciousness and earth-life requires an acceptance of the femine aspect of creation. Herein we have the essence of *Tantra*–instead of drawing back from Nature and its difficulties, *Tantra* accepts and transforms Nature into its pure essence–God. Rather than recoiling from life, the Tantric yogi embraces all of existence, including earthly life, as a manifestation and reality of God.

As with all philosophy, ideas are often manipulated and deformed so as to suit the various desires of those seeking justification for their actions. This fate has befallen the philosophy of *Tantra*–which has, at the abysmal depths of misunderstanding, become known as the *yoga* of sex. This misconception is perpetrated by careless teachers and writers who put forth ancient sculptures, writings and paintings depicting sexual acts as a validation of "sex-*yoga*." I cringe at the possibilities of future generations or cultures putting forward our culture's pornographic literature and photography as a validation for more of the same. Let us leave behind these immature interpretations which have mistaken indulgence for acceptance and understanding.

The Tantric yogi sees and feels God in every atom of earth existence. While others claim life to be the dance of illusion and falsehood, the practitioner of *Tantra* cannot conceive of God's earth-creation as anything other than God. Those who wish to transform earth-existence into its fullest and greatest potential must accept the earth-creation as God and then allow for the descent of the infinite into the finite. The first step in this process is the transformation of one's own life and consciousness.

This transformation is effected by the surrender of our lower nature, which is dominated by our egotistic, divisionary view of reality, to our higher nature which is characterized by an aspiration for perfection in the pure awareness and experience of the oneness of God manifested in the multiplicity of creation. This passage from our lower nature to our higher nature is the essence of the spiritual journey.

If one's goal is to escape from the world to find and experience God then there is no necessity for the transformation of nature. If, however, we choose to not only find God but also to bring about the manifestation of God upon earth in and through our own existence, then the acceptance of the creative aspect of life is essential.

It is important to remember that there is a vast difference between the transformation of our lower nature and indulgence in our lower nature. The deformation of Tantric philosophy occurs because indulgence is substituted for transformation. The process of *Tantra* begins with acceptance. Acceptance brings a clear vision and knowledge of our needs and desires; we must understand the intricate workings of that which we seek to change and transform. Once this clear awareness has been attained there is a tremendous temptation to then utilize this knowledge in order to derive the utmost pleasure and power for oneself. This is indulgence. The sincere seeker of God will not choose to utilize this awareness for egocentric satisfaction but will instead use this understanding and clarity to ensure the complete transformation and utilization of the lower nature into and by the higher nature which is the all-pervading unity of existence. In this way the seeker's earthly energy and power can be effectively used to first establish the presence of God in the terrestial life of the seeker and then, through all available avenues, to offer this consciousness to others as an inspiration and aid in their own efforts towards and into the Infinite and Eternal.

In the process of the spiritual journey, many are the seekers who have come to a deep understanding of themselves and their inner workings. Unfortunatley this knowledge easily converts to power which can be used to manipulate others in an effort to attain more power and pleasure. Many individuals who seek to pass themselves off as spiritual teachers are, in reality, not true spiritual teachers, but rather men and women who have attained some psychic or occult power and then use this power to attract attention and the adoration and money of unwise seekers. The only protection against such people and the devastating experiences they bring to those who fall prey to their tricks is the seeker's heartfelt sincerity.

Ultimately, each of us, in the process of our spiritual journey, will come to the point when we have mastered our lower nature and have to decide which path we shall choose–the path of earthly egocentric power or the path of oneness, transformation and God-manifestation. Let us make a wise choice. All of existence, including God, is watching.

By studying the ancient arts of *yoga* we can more perfectly understand the essence of spiritual practice. This balanced understanding is essential for us to journey to an awareness of God.

In the past seekers were encouraged to choose one form of *yoga*. The idea of integral *yoga* is to integrate all methods and not to limit ourselves to a particular one. Every day situations provide avenues for inner growth and self-knowledge. We can learn to see success and failure, happiness and sorrow, not as end-experiences, but rather as opportunities for learning, understanding, and self-transcendence.

Daily meditation helps us find a calm and quiet space within ourselves from which to experience life. It is a time for us to focus our thoughts and awareness, quiet our mind and find our center in peace. Through a wholehearted acceptance of life we realize that every day, every moment, every interaction, and every relationship that we feel, that we experience, is an opportunity for self-growth and understanding. It is an opportunity for *yoga.*

It is important that we allow ourselves space for our regular daily meditation, at least 5 to 10 minutes each day. Our sincere daily effort will assure us of feelings and experiences beyond our imagination. Imagination is limited to mind. The experiences attainable through meditation transcend the mind. Meditation is our awareness of God and the universal consciousness which is beyond the grasp of our human mind.

Our task is to create the opportunity within our day for the mystical thoughts, feelings, inspirations and aspirations of spirituality to enter into our consciousness. The expectaction of a certain experience from meditation often limits our receptivity because we are limiting ourselves to expectations created by our minds.

Meditation involves cultivating an awareness of our inner significance. By sitting quietly each day we offer the infinite consciousness of existence the chance to permeate and transform our human, limited consciousness into the unlimited consciousness of Immortality. As a beautiful flower opens to the sun and blooms into unforseen beauty, so too shall our finite, earthbound consciousness flower into an expanse unimaginable.

Section II

Getting Started with Meditation

WHEN THE MIND IS RIGHT

When the mind is right
When it is light
Can look at itself and laugh
Be silly or funny or sad
In a moment change
Or accept a new idea–
When the mind is like that
Life is a breeze.
Like wind through the trees
Blowing leaves
In so many directions
Missing all the connections
But somehow finding its way
Exactly to where...
It was meant to go.

When the mind is bright
Allowing in the light
Creating space
Like a sun-filled room
It's then, windows open,
That things happen, develop, change.

To win or lose at money or romance
Doesn't affect the internal dance
The energy flowing, the life going
So fast, so quickly through these...
Open windows and doors.

8

The Basics

Daily Meditation

Through meditation we explore a depth of awareness concerning ourselves, our lives and the world that would otherwise be rarely accessed. The daily practice of meditation allows us time for self-reflection and contemplation. We are able to ask ourselves deep questions about who we are, what we are and why we are here. Meditation gives us the opportunity and space to inquire into ourselves, into our lives, into our existence. Meditation is a profound experience. It is not a method of building up our ego, but rather a time of spiritual awakening, of letting go of our deep-rooted sense of separativity and experienceing our intrinsic oneness with all of existence. Eventually, with persistence and determination we are able to touch the source of all creation. We consciously enter into the core of humanity's quest from the beginning of time: Who am I? Where have I come from? What is my purpose? Who is my creator? The daily practice of meditation gives us an opportunity to pursue these questions.

Our own daily meditation also has an effect upon the world. The world is intricately woven. In a vibrant web of energy everything is interconnected. If you are able to achieve a calm and quiet mind, you will be bringing peacefulness, calmness, tolerance and beauty into the world and this will affect everyone else in this intricately woven web of existence. By reading the newspaper and watching the news, you can see that peace, harmony and oneness are seldom experienced in our modern world. Our world is full of hatred, jealousy, anger, resentment, war, and conflict; these powers also have an effect upon each one of us. What type of energy do you want to be responsible for bringing into the earth consciousness? Each thought, feeling and action of ours is a creation. Each one of us, everyday, is creating the world of tomorrow.

It is said that many saints and yogis have spent their entire lives meditating in solitude for world peace, for humanity's growth towards an awareness of God and Truth. Daily prayer and meditation is our opportunity to touch our spirits, our souls, and bring that energy into our world.

Choose a part of your day that you can set aside for daily meditation. By practicing meditation each day we develop an awareness and strength for spiritual experiences. Our daily meditation is our preparation of the soil into which the universe can plant its seeds of consciousness. By meditating 10 minutes each day we will, after one year, have meditated over 60 hours. The power of daily practice quickly adds up.

Beginning

When meditating, it is important to stay awake. I suggest sitting up straight during meditation, whether in a chair or sitting cross-legged on the floor. It is essential that the spine remain as straight as is comfortable. With practice, as your back becomes stronger, you will be able to sit straighter and for longer periods of time. During meditation, as higher qualities enter into us, or emerge from within us, a straight spine is important for the harmonious flow of this new energy throughout our body.

Many of the exercises that you will learn to calm and quiet your mind can be used at night to help you fall asleep. At that time, you will be lying down. But, when we decide that we are going to meditate, we do not want to enter the world of sleep. Another technique, to ensure that we don't sleep, is to keep our eyes slightly open. With the eyes half open, we maintain a connection with what we are experiencing in our meditation and, at the same time, are aware of the physical world. In this way we are able to experience an integrated reality. Oftentimes, when closing our eyes, we drift into daydreams or into sleep, and upon returning to waking consciousness we may doubt our inner experiences, writing them off as mere daydreams. By keeping our eyes halfway open we assure ourselves of the validity of our inner experiences.

Individual and Group

There are two basic settings in which meditation can be done: by yourself or with others. Both are necessary for balanced spiritual growth. Meditating by ourselves offers us an opportunity to meditate free from the distractions of others, at a time and place most suitable for us. Group meditation also has its benefits. During meditation we become conscious of realms of subtle energy which are accessible only as we quiet our thoughts and bring peace into our being. When we sit side-by-side with others during meditation, their inspiration and aspiration will nurture our own meditation. The energy that we create and offer into the universe each time we sit down to meditate is powerful and significant, and should never be underestimated.

We all share an underlying unity of consciousness. By joining together with others in meditation, our awareness of this connectedness is strenghtened and we are able to strengthen our offering to the world. According to ancient scriptures, the strength of group meditation is intensified greatly when twelve or more people join together.

For individual meditation, five to ten minutes a day, everyday, is all that is needed in the beginning. The guide for your meditation should always be your own happiness–the joy you are receiving from your practice. By making a daily effort you create the opportunity for the spirit within yourself to come forward.

Some days you will have "good meditations," and other days it will be more difficult to feel that peace and calm. Regardless of our daily circumstances and schedule changes, we must give ourselves the opportunity for meditation. On certain days we may cultivate or become aware of a profound sense of peace and calmness during our meditation. At those times there is no reason to end our meditation just because a certain amount of time has elapsed. Allow your meditation to expand, both inwardly–in terms of depth, and outwardly–in terms of length of time. Meditation is expansion in both the inner and outer world. If during a particular meditation you find it impossible to calm your mind, then there is no harm in simply reading a spiritual book, a book you find inspiring; listening to some peaceful music, or focusing on a positive thought or idea. You can even repeat aloud to yourself a statement such as, "I am part and parcel of the infinite," or other empowering statements or *mantras.* We must be flexible and adaptable in our practice, not rigid and uncreative.

Weekly group meditation, because of the strength of the group consciousness, can last twice or even three times the length of an individual's daily practice. Group meditation can include readings from sacred scriptures, offered aloud, to focus the group awareness and direction. The same applies to music, singing and chanting–all of these activities help to align the consciousness of the entire group.

Where

Ideally we should have a regular place for our individual meditation, whether it is a corner of our room, an entire room in our home, a park bench or any place where we can go and be free of distractions. The reason for this is twofold: by consistently meditating there, having this sacred spot for our practice, we create a meditative vibration in that area. We create an energy. Every time we sit down to meditate that energy becomes stronger. Secondly, just as we have various rooms in our house—when we go into the breakfast room, we know we will eat breakfast; when we go into our bedroom, we will sleep—so, too, when we go into our meditation area we know exactly what will take place in that room: meditation. We want to make that place free from distractions: ringing telephone, other people, television, and other common distractions.

In the place where you practice your daily meditation it is essential to create an altar or shrine towards which you can focus your attention when practising your meditation. On your shrine you can place objects which will inspire you, remind you of your own spiritual journey and be practical aids in your practice. I suggest: candles, flowers, incense, photographs (either of people or places that offer you spiritual inspiration), uplifting music and books. In essence you are creating your own church or sacred, holy ground where you can commune with the spirit and potential within and around you. Freed from the pull of the mundane, your consciousness can dance with the limitless aspect of existence. You can then infuse this new energy and feeling into your daily activities. I know a number of individuals who use the daily practice of meditation as an oasis amidst the intensity of their business careers. They enjoy the focus and concentration needed in their careers. They also find it essential to meditate and infuse the intensity with joy and gratitude which they derive from their meditation.

By creating this sacred spot you are also saying to yourself and those who know you: "The spiritual quest is a reality for me and this is the sacred area where I sit to seek and know the vastness of all that is."

For group meditation, it would be ideal if an entire room of the home could be set aside just for the practice of meditation. A large shrine can be placed at the front of the room. Light, soothing colors on the walls, ceiling and carpet will help to awaken and enliven the consciousness of all meditating. A well lit room will aid in keeping everyone awake. Candles, flowers, incense, inspirational music and readings will uplift the group's aspiration. It should be remembered by all in the group that oneness and equality are the cornerstones of balanced growth. All who seek God will come to find God as part and parcel of themselves and others, therefore all are equal, for all are one.

When

Anytime we are able to meditate is the best time for meditation. In our hectic society with busy schedules, work and a myriad of responsibilities, just finding five to ten minutes a day for meditation is an accomplishment. What is most important is that you do practice, every day.

If you are able to accommodate your schedule or make changes, there are certain times in the day that are more conducive to meditation. These times coincide with the cycles of nature. Morning is a splendid time for meditation. When we wake, the sun is rising, the new day is dawning. Nature is once again beginning her growth process, the sun is beginning to shine; this is an excellent time for meditation. The dawning of the day reminds us—inspires us—of the dawning of our own consciousness and the dawning of our aspiration for the soulful and spiritual experiences life can offer us.

Noon is a powerful time to meditate. With the sun at its apex we find the world fully active and dynamic. Meditation is not just the experience of peace and calm; meditation also embodies the dynamic and powerful. Noon—the middle of the day—is a time of power for nature and we can feel that power within our own consciousness.

In the evening, as the sun is setting, the world is again in transition; we leave behind our multifarious activities, the hustle and bustle, and we enter into the calm of the evening. This aspect of day allows us the opportunity to let go of problems, worries and anxieties and enter into the quiet, soulful peace of evening.

Before going to sleep at night is another excellent time for a few moments of meditation. This is the time to calm and quiet our mind and body before going to sleep. Sleep is a significant part of our lives; in fact, it is a sort of biological meditation, and by preparing ourselves and infusing ourselves with a peaceful consciousness, we create a deeper, more fulfilling and effective sleep.

Midnight is a soulful time for meditation on the quality of love. Love begins with self-acceptance. Concentrate and meditate upon a photograph of yourself which you feel embodies your best qualities. While concentrating on your photograph allow your body and mind to relax. Becoming comfortable with your image in the photograph helps you to accept and love yourself. Once we feel love within ourselves we have access to the greatest thing we can offer to others: love.

Finally, 3 a.m. is called the hour of *Brahma,* or the hour of God. If you have ever awakened at 3 a.m., you will find the earth consciousness silent and asleep, deep within the peace of rest. By meditating at 3 a.m., we are able to enter into that peacefulness, that calmness.

Of all the times mentioned, the most practical are in the morning and in the evening. When meditating in the morning we gather peacefulness and calmness into ourselves and are then able to access these qualities during our day. It is as if we are putting money in the bank and during the day we draw from our account. When we face stressful situations we can use the peace and quiet and power from our morning meditation to deal with these challenging moments. During the evening meditation we can invoke peace and then reflect on our day, resolving events that we have pushed away from our consciousness. As our day's activities and memories melt into peace we are renewed and ready to experience the evening hours.

Assimilation

After meditation we want to assimilate our meditation-energy into our normal consciousness. If we feel peace, relaxation and harmony during our meditation, we try to hold on to these feelings after we finish meditation and once again enter into our daily activities. We must aspire to assimilate the inner awareness of meditation with our outer awareness of the objective world. This is no easy task, and yet, the ability to bring spiritual awareness and feelings into our everyday waking consciousness is one of the most powerful experiences in life.

As we learn to infuse this peaceful awareness into our life, we will find other people becoming aware of our peacefulness, of our calmness, of our happiness. Everyone wants to be happy. We all pursue it in various ways, through various activities, goals and aspirations. If we strive to cultivate happiness within ourselves, and we project that happiness into our lives, we will find people drawn to us. This reality, this undercurrent of happiness will affect, in a positive way, all aspects of our lives. Therefore, assimilation of that peace and calm is an essential part of our daily practice.

In the beginning, holding onto the feeling you experience in your meditation for more than fifteen or twenty minutes after meditation may be difficult. Eventually, the day will dawn when that awareness of your inner poise will permeate every waking moment of your life.

9

Focusing

One of the goals of the meditation practice is to see reality clearly, to see our lives clearly, without the debris of unwanted thoughts. The first step in learning meditation is to confront this maze of thought by learning to focus our minds on one object, whether a sound, sight, feeling, image, thought or movement. The object upon which we concentrate should be something we find inspiring and uplifting. Through regular practice we slowly and steadily bring stillness to our mind. This stillness embodies peace and calm.

It is through our minds, primarily, that we perceive reality. Our thoughts create our reality.

A sunset to one person can be the height of beauty while that same sunset to another can represent tremendous sorrow. It is the same sunset, yet to each individual it is a different event based on the thoughts influencing their mind and perceptions at that moment.

The mind can be equated with the surface of a lake on a windy day. The wind, an everyday occurrence, stirs up the surface of the lake, causing waves and ripples. This is analogous to the condition of our minds blown by the winds of thought. Through meditation and concentration we learn to calm the thought-winds, bringing a stillness to our minds. When the lake is calm, we are able to look down and perceive its true depths. Likewise, when our mind is calm, we are able to perceive our spirit's depth, the depth of our being, the silence and stillness of our soul. When the lake is calm, you can also see the reflection of all that surrounds the lake: the mountains, the sky and the trees. By creating stillness and calm in our minds, we are able to perceive more clearly the people, events and situations that surround us, since our perception is less influenced by our skewed thoughts, by the waves on the surface of the lake.

In an effort to achieve this clear perception, we must begin by calming the mind, by learning to focus on one object. The only requirement for an object of concentration is that it be simple and calming. It is helpful if it is connected with nature. Focus and concentrate on a flower, fountain, candle flame, your breath, pulse or the sound of a beautiful instrument—something simple and calming. By sitting and focusing on that object for a few minutes, we will soon find calmness and stillness entering into our minds.

As soon as you begin to focus you will immediately become aware of distracting thoughts. Do not be judgemental of yourself when this happens. Do not consider this as an indication that you cannot learn concentration and meditation. Everyone, the world over, has this experience when first learning meditation. Just observing your thoughts and being aware of your thinking process is a significant achievement, for it indicates that a deeper part of you is becoming conscious and observing the thought-process. Most people are seemingly trapped in their thought-reality. You are developing the awareness of a higher aspect of yourself. When your awareness is pulled away by thought, simply return your awareness to the object of concentration as soon as you become aware that you have lost your focus. Slowly and steadily, through this practice, you will become the master of your thoughts and break the shackles which thoughts, regardless of their origin, place on your perceptions and hence, your life and actions.

You will find that while concentrating you become aware of many thoughts. Merely try to put as much awareness on the object of concentration as is possible and comfortable. Thousands of thoughts, or the potential for thousands of thoughts, exist within your mind at any given moment. Thoughts of the future, thoughts of the past, thoughts of the present—all of these pass through your mind at any given moment. Our goal in the beginning stages of meditation is to learn to focus and concentrate as much of our awareness on a single point as possible.

Concentration is often equated with an arrow, signifying single-pointed attention. With the power of concentration, with the single-pointedness of that arrow, we will be able to pierce through the maze of our thoughts. Every day we must spend five minutes on a focusing exercise as part of our daily meditation practice.

The method or object of concentration is of secondary importance. It is the effect that you receive from the concentration that is important. There are many types of concentration practices in which our focus is directed towards various points. The important thing is for you to find a few exercises that resonate with your awareness. Some people may be drawn to music or sound; other people may be more visual; some will prefer an awareness of breath, pulse or heart-beat; and still others may find it easier to concentrate on something within their own minds, for example, the image of a flower or the visualization of a peaceful, calm lake. Regardless of what the object of concentration is, we want to focus our attention on it fully. If your concentration effort makes you feel tension or any kind of stress, you are pushing yourself too hard. Always remember this basic premise: peace and calm are the foundations of a healthy meditation practice. If we get headaches or stress through concentration, either we are not doing it correctly or we are pushing ourselves beyond our capacity. From true concentration and focusing we will get a feeling of calmness and eventually an ever-increasing identification with the object of concentration.

EXERCISE 3

Find a comfortable place where you can quietly sit. For five minutes simply concentrate on a single object—a flower or candle flame. Keep your gaze focused yet not rigid or uncomfortable. Another time focus on your breath; merely watch your body breathe. You can also focus on simple sounds, for example, the ocean waves, wind whistling through trees, or music which has been specifically designed for meditation. Do not be critical of yourself if your attention drifts away; simply return your awareness to your object of concentration as soon as possible.

Try to practice some form of concentration each day. With time and practice, your ability to focus and concentrate will increase. The potential is there; you only need to develop and cultivate that which is your birthright: a calm and peaceful awareness.

As your ability to concentrate increases you will find different powers developing within yourself. First, through concentration, you will be able to fully identify with anything upon which you concentrate. Through this process you are able to perceive the essence of the object and hence, concentration brings knowledge.

Secondly, through sincere and single-minded concentration you can acquire any object that you desire.

Finally, by concentration on your ideal self and life, you can become that upon which you concentrate.

10

Relaxation

Once we have learned to calm and quiet our mind, to bring our consciousness to a point of focus, then we can focus on bringing peace, tranquility, and harmony into our lives. We can begin this process by bringing relaxation and calmness into our bodies.

Relaxation is very important. The calm and peace of the body will benefit our health and provide us the energy necessary for daily meditation and all of the activities in which we find ourselves involved. After we have learned to bring ourselves to a focused awareness, we can invoke relaxation and calmness into our being.

To begin this process it is not necessary that every single thought in our mind be eliminated. Rather, through the concentration and focusing exercises, we learn to focus intently, so that we can give power to a chosen object, thought, image or ideal. In the case of relaxation we will focus on calmness and stillness in our breathing and the relaxation of our body through visualization. This is not relaxation to help you fall asleep—although these exercises can be done at night, while lying in bed to help you fall asleep. In this type of meditative relaxation you are sitting up straight and bringing calmness and stillness into the body. When the body is calm we are able to focus our awareness on deeper and higher realms of consciousness. In contrast, when our body is agitated and restless our awareness is trapped—like a caged bird—in the physical realm. When our bodies are calm our consciousness is able to fly to higher sources of energy. Once we connect with these higher realms we are able to bring the energy found there into our physical body for health and into our mind and heart for inspiration and motivation.

EXERCISE 4

Begin by sitting quietly, focusing on your breath. Watch your body breathe. Be aware of each inhalation and each exhalation and the way your body moves as you breathe. If possible breathe in and out through your nose, pausing for a fraction of a second between each inhalation and exhalation. After 3 or 4 minutes, each time you breathe in, imagine you are breathing in peace and calm. As you exhale, feel your body relaxing; imagine the muscles in your body becoming calm and relaxed. Focus especially on the muscles in your forehead, around your eyes, in the back of the neck and shoulders. In these muscles we carry much of our stress—emotional, mental, and physical. Hence, by consciously relaxing these muscle groups we release the psychological tension which created the muscular tension. This psychological tension is absorbed and illumined by the conscious feeling of stillness and peace which we are bringing into our consciousness during meditation. Breathe in peace, exhale and allow these muscle groups to relax. Try this for 5 to 10 minutes.

11

Peace

Peace begins to well up within our consciousness as we clear away distracting thoughts, anxieties and worries. For thousands of years spiritual teachers appearing in different times and cultures have repeatedly expressed the same essential message: within each of us exists a spark of the Infinite and Eternal. Within this spark exists peace in boundless measure. One of the most tangible aspects of this light within us is the feeling of peace and calm that begins to shine within our consciousness as we still our restless body and mind.

A quiet walk on the beach, an afternoon spent gardening, offering our help to others, moments of quiet contemplation—all of these activities embody the essence of meditation and help to open our inner consciousness, our inner awareness, which in time, brings peace. As we quiet our minds, we will find peace. Every thorn we remove from our foot brings a sense of relief, so too, every day that we meditate, we transcend or let go of a certain worry or thought or an aspect of our identity that is not productive. This brings the experience of peace. Every day that we are able to allow a little peace to emerge within our consciousness is sure to be a day of soulful satisfaction.

It often happens that distracting or negative thoughts arise during the meditative practice. Do not be discouraged by their presence. This happens to everyone. You have been thinking for many years. To silence the mind, to awaken the spiritual heart, does not happen overnight. Be patient and persistent. During meditation the intensity of thought is tenfold. A thought that we have in passing, while involved in multifarious activities has very little power. But when we are silent and calm, our mind serene, that same thought can have tremendous power. The force of our concentration is immense. Therefore, while concentrating and meditating we need to be careful to guard our consciousness from negative or destructive thoughts. It is as if you were at the front door of your home. Inside are things and people important to you: your children and family, things that you own and value. Naturally you guard your home from troublesome strangers. When people come to your door, you are not going to allow just anyone into your home. You will not allow entrance to a visitor whom you feel might be destructive or harmful. In the same way, we do our best to watch carefully those thoughts which we allow into our minds during meditation. We should not allow negative thoughts, self-deprecating images, thoughts of self-doubt and painful memories into our minds during meditation. This type of energy will not be helpful or productive in our lives. Those thoughts are not helpful in our day to day existence, we assuredly do not want to magnify and intensify them during meditation.

Sometimes during my meditation negative thoughts or images arise which I am not able, at that time, to stop. Such being the case, I will end my meditation thereby diffusing the meditation/concentration energy which would have intensified those thoughts and images.

With time and the practice of meditation the peace you learn to cultivate will act as a powerful fire which will destroy all negative thoughts.

Earlier I noted that meditation is an inclusive activity which accepts life in all its diversity and multiplicity. Here, in this chapter, you are advised to be selective regarding what is allowed into your consciousness. By being selective we are not rejecting or denying aspects of our existence; we are simply being wise in admitting the limits of our capacity to deal with certain aspects of our consciousness at any given time. Eventually we will not only come to know and accept all aspects of our existence but also transform every aspect to embody its greatest potential and capacity. In meditation we must always try to focus on the highest thoughts, feelings and ideals that we can perceive. Even in a large, dark room, where no light exists, a single match can illumine the darkness. So too, our minds and lives are full of complexities, full of problems, and yet, through our daily practice of meditation, we can light a candle of peace, of happiness, of joy, of gratitude, that will eventually illumine our entire life. The meditation period is an opportunity to cultivate that light and peace within ourselves.

EXERCISE 5

Begin by focusing on your breath, a candle or a flower for 2–3 minutes. Now close your eyes and bring into your mind a scene from nature (either create one or remember a place you have been) that for you evokes a feeling of peace. Each time you breathe in, imagine you are breathing in the calm essence from that scene; feel it gradually permeating your body with each breath. With each exhalation feel the muscles in your body becoming loose and relaxed. After you can feel a tangible peace and calm within yourself let go of the image and simply focus on the peace and calm within your consciousness.

When visualizing the image your eyes will be closed. You want to "see" the image as large and as clearly as possible–as if you were looking up at a mural on the side of a building, a large painting in a museum or a movie screen. Everyone benefits from a large and clear visual image. Other variables such as whether the image is in color or black and white, moving or still, with or without sound and smells will depend on individual preferences. There is also the factor of whether you are in the image, a part of the scene, or an observer of the image. To determine the particulars for yourself take a moment and visually remember something pleasant that has happenead to you recently. Note how you are visualizing, how you "see" the scene. Now apply these same aspects to your image of peace or any visual image to which you wish to give strength.

12

Guided Imagery

All the man-made things which we see around us began with imagination—someone imagined something and then took the necessary steps to create it. Chairs, buildings, bridges, water systems, computer systems, airplanes, rockets, cities, works of art, books—all of these things began in a human being's mind, in a human being's imagination. Visualization can also be applied to creating, directing and expanding our life's potential. Before people achieve something they envision the possibility within their own mind and then work towards that end. Some reach their goals, their dreams, others do not;

regardless of the outcome, they envision and strive. Martin Luther King exemplifies this in his "I have a dream..." speech.

How we think of ourselves dictates the person we are. What we imagine ourselves to be greatly defines what we can become. We can use this knowledge in practical ways during our daily meditation practice. If we perceive a quality in nature, such as harmony, and we feel a lack of harmony within ourselves, we can use creative visualization to bring more harmony into our lives.

Anything that we can perceive in the world is perceptible to us only because we possess that very quality within ourselves. We cannot be aware of things that we do not ourselves already possess. If we feel some peace within, we can see peace in nature. If we feel love, we can share that love and we can see that love in others. When we see harmony in nature, it is because this harmony exists within ourselves.

When following this line of thought it is fascinating to wonder about what we are capable of perceiving. Men and women who have dedicated their lives to an understanding of life and God–a dedication any of us can choose– repeatedly tell us that inside each individual lies all of existence. Try to imagine that person's awareness of life. Let their achievement be an inspiration to your own practice of meditation.

We often think of life as consisting of our inner, or psychological life, and the outer, or material life. Yet, some profess that these are not separate, but rather one. Based on this it would follow that the more we know of ourselves, and our inner workings, the more we thereby know of time, space and the whole of life itself.

Through this knowledge we can bring into our lives qualities which we feel will make our lives more satisfying. For example, you could choose to bring more simplicity, sincerity, purity, sweetness, compassion, confidence, dynamism, love and acceptance into your life. Try devoting a few months to each of these qualities, one at a time. The results will amaze you.

This knowledge can also be used to alleviate the stress or conflict that may arise in certain situations which we confront in the course of our day. If we know that on a particular day we will have a stressful encounter with a work associate or acquaintance, we can imagine the encounter taking place, but see ourself as interacting peacefully and staying well-poised within the situation. Through positive visualization of the event beforehand, we can alter our usual behavior patterns and open ourselves to new possibilities. It is by becoming conscious and aware of the vast potential within ourselves that we are able to create change in our lives.

By utilizing the power of visualization and imagination, we begin to open ourselves to untold potential. Creative visualization is a skill that can be applied to all aspects of our lives, from developing positive qualities to creative problem solving. With practice, we will develop an awareness that is only limited by the boundaries we place upon ourselves. Creative visualization helps us to break through these barriers and expand our latent potential.

EXERCISE 6

Begin with 3–5 minutes of relaxation and concentration. Next, bring to mind a quality you wish to cultivate. Repeat the name of this quality to yourself for a few minutes and then imagine a scene from nature (you can either make one up or choose a place you have been) that for you represents this quality. Whenever I visualize the quality of confidence I choose to imagine a powerful waterfall. See and feel in that scene the quality you have chosen. Once you have a good visual image then each time you breathe in feel that you are breathing in the quality from that image. As you exhale, feel that your body is becoming calm and relaxed. Breathe in the quality, breathe out and allow your body to relax. Continue this exercise for 3-5 minutes. To end, open your eyes allowing the image to dissolve yet keep the feeling of the quality strong in your awareness. The next time you feel a need for this quality recall the image and bring forward the feeling and quality you have now associated with this image. In this way, with practice, you can bring any quality or energy into your life.

EXERCISE 7

Once you have focused, relaxed and brought forward a feeling of peace, imagine yourself in a difficult or tense situation that you have been in or will be in, but visualize yourself as calm and poised. See and feel yourself reacting to the people or situation with peace of mind. Train yourself through guided imagery to be the person you want to be. You should be the artist of your own life-picture. In this particular exercise it is essential to have a solid base of peace in your consciousness so as not to be initially overwhelmed by the visual image of a situation that is a challenge to you. Your sense of peace–derived from meditation–is the key element to opening your awareness to the potential for new possibilities.

13

Higher Emotions

As part of the meditation practice we learn to first focus on a predominant object or thought; we then learn to bring peace and calm into our being, and finally, if we are prepared, we can take a truly evolutionary leap in consciousness. A leap virtually undreamed of by most of humanity. This leap of awareness is achieved by our awareness of higher emotions.

Most often meditation is described or explained as relating to the mind–quieting the mind, stilling thought, etc. Yet meditation embodies a transformation and utilization of our emotional nature as well. Emotions span a vast spectrum including depression, sorrow, anger, fear, jealously, excitement, enthusiasm, happiness, compassion, love and gratitude. We are all well aware of the "lower" emotions such as sorrow, anger and jealousy. It is in the realm of higher emotions–love, compassion and gratitude–that we can experience levels of awareness and satisfaction of which we now possess only a glimpse. Meditation will provide us the avenues to explore these emotions and bring these realities into the earth-consciousness.

Allow me to illustrate the power of higher emotions. We have all had days when our mood turns sour, when we are unhappy and then, quite unexpectedly, we run into a good friend or receive a nice letter or telephone call. The good news or pleasant encounter brings us joy and happiness and by focusing on this joy we quickly overcome or transform the sorrow of a previous moment. In a split second our consciousness can change by identifying with higher emotions–such as our feelings for our friend or good news received. This transformation did not take place by eliminating all thought; rather it took place because we focused or allowed a higher emotion to wipe clean the slate of our consciousness, to take us to a higher, more vast level of awareness.

One of the most powerful and transforming of these higher emotions is that of gratitude. We all know the feeling of gratitude and the lightness and joy it brings to our entire being. Many are the reasons for our gratitude. One of the most profound, yet sublime, reasons for gratitude is the simple fact of being alive.

To cultivate a feeling of gratitude for our very existence is a profound experience that can change our lives. Two other emotions that are spiritually powerful are the feeling of oneness with humanity and a feeling of compassion for other people, in fact, for all of existence.

True compassion is not based on self-interest or on a feeling of being superior to someone else. True compassion is based on the awareness that we are all part and parcel of the same existence: the earth, the trees, the animals, the humans–all aspects of existence are interrelated and dependent upon one another.

Higher emotions can awaken a spirit, a depth within ourselves, that is not ascertainable through the mind and thinking process. The driving force of life is evolution, both physical and spiritual. Humanity is evolving from the mental realm into the realm of these higher emotions. If you observe others you will see that some people are more connected with feelings of gratitude, oneness and compassion than others. One man may spend his life serving his own senses; another will offer his very life so that others may live more fulfilling lives. Through the meditative process you can increase your own evolution of consciousness tenfold by consciously making an effort to realize and manifest love, compassion and gratitude in your own life.

EXERCISE 8

Begin by calming and quieting your body and mind for 3–5 minutes. Focus and relax. Next choose something for which you are grateful, whether it is a place, person, relationship, situation or possession. Focus as entirely as possible on that object. In doing this you will begin to feel gratitude within yourself. Focus on this feeling and allow it to expand through your body, emotional being and mind.

14

The Heart Center

After having read and meditated upon many books on the topics of spirituality, religion and meditation, I have come to realize that one of the essential feelings to create in life is a feeling of oneness: the interconnectedness of all of creation. From a recognition of this oneness can blossom the true powers of the soul: humility; compassion; and delight.

It has been written time and time again, and has been the realization of many spiritual teachers, that this all-encompassing oneness is to be found, or its potential is said to reside, in the center of the chest–in the heart center.

We all possess the potential energy necessary for this expansion of consciousness. One of the most rewarding spiritual disciplines is the process of opening and expanding the energy of the heart center. This is done through concentration, visualization and meditation. The spiritual heart is said to be the seat of the soul and the energy realm from which mind and intellect come forth. In the Upanishads, ancient scripture from India, it is written:

> *"He [God] envelopes the universe. Though transcendent, He is to be meditated upon as residing in the lotus of the heart, at the center of the body, ten fingers above the navel. Smaller than the smallest, greater than the greatest, the Self is hidden in the heart of all creatures."*

The exercise in this chapter is intended to increase an awareness of the heart center. By becoming aware of this heart-center of consciousness within our being we gain access to the transcendent reality from which all creation has come forth.

The heart center is the safest energy center to open to begin our spiritual journey. All of the energy centers have various powers connected with them, yet without the wisdom of our heart center, it is often dangerous to access these powers. A knife will provide us an excellent metaphor for power. With a knife we can cut up a piece of fruit and share it with our friends, or we can kill somebody. In both cases we are using the same knife. The deciding factor is the wisdom, or lack thereof, with which we use the knife. Spiritual, psychic and occult powers are much like worldly powers. Money is a power. Position in society is power. How we use any type of power depends on our wisdom. There is nothing inherently wrong or evil with power, yet, when people do not have the wisdom or the knowledge of how to use power, there is sure to be trouble. The destruction of others and often the destruction of the possessor of the power, soon ensues.

In order to find and nourish the heart center energy one of the main qualities which you need to cultivate is purity. The foundation of our spiritual growth is purity. Purity in thought, word and deed. It is for good reason that Jesus said, "Blessed are the pure in heart for they shall see God."

Pure thoughts are those which center upon kindness, love, compassion, oneness, gratitude, God and other such ideas and energies. Impure thoughts are those which take our mind away from these energies. Purity of heart encompasses purity of thought and also includes purity of emotion. Pure emotions are those emotions which create within us a deep longing for God and Truth.

Purity in mind and heart embodies qualities such as fearlessness, vastness and independence. Pure thoughts and feelings allow our minds and hearts to expand and open into realms of awareness unavailable to those whose minds and hearts are cluttered and heavy with the weight of impurity.

Meditation on the heart center helps us to cultivate the wisdom and understanding that can bring us into closer harmony with ourselves and with our truest nature, the nature that feels oneness: oneness in unity, multiplicity and diversity.

EXERCISE 9

Begin with concentrating and relaxing for five minutes. Then imagine a beautiful rose or flower in its bud form, located in the center of your chest. Feel and imagine that each time you breathe in, the incoming energy helps the flower to slowly blossom, petal by petal. As you exhale imagine that you are offering the fragrance, beauty and purity of the flower, which is none other than your own blossoming inner beauty, to those you truly love and cherish in your heart. You can also imagine the heart center as a ball of white or gold light, or as a feeling of love and compassion. Imagine that each incoming breath increases the beauty, light, love or compassion. Try this exercise for 5 to 10 minutes. By using creative visualization, we open our awareness to the subtle energies and emotions in our being. Breathe in and allow the image in your heart center to grow and expand.

15

Teachers

As mentioned in the preface, the guidance of a true, genuine, spiritual teacher is an integral part of the meditative experience. Ultimately, no one can tell you who is the right teacher for you. Only you can know your teacher.

A true spiritual teacher is a person, a man or woman, who inspires you in your own inner growth. A spiritual teacher is someone who has plunged to the depths, and climbed to the heights of human potential and returned to offer others the inspiration to undertake that same journey for themselves.

In Sanskrit, the ancient language of India, the term "Guru" literally means, "he who dispels darkness." In our journey into consciousness, the aid of a teacher is invaluable. In all that we seek to understand in life we enlist the help of teachers, whether it is our first grade teacher helping us with the alphabet, a philosophy professor in college or a grandparent disseminating wisdom into our lives. Regardless of what we wish to learn, the aid of a teacher is undoubtedly invaluable. It is our wisdom and intelligence that enlists the guidance of one wiser, whether in the study of philosophy, science, or spirituality.

When a true spiritual teacher is found, the help and guidance is unimaginable. A true teacher offers inspiration to the seeker, both mental inspiration through writings or teaching, and inspiration on a personal level. In a true teacher one sees one's goal; one sees the reality of the fact that everyone possesses the Infinite. A teacher is the living embodiment of that reality. True spiritual teachers are powerful, significant individuals.

If we look at the world around us, at the world's great religions, we see that each of these religions began with a single man or woman. The power of their convictions, understanding and insights into the realities of life provided the basis of what are now worldwide religions. Obviously, to encounter such an individual is both a blessing and a significant opportunity.

We can see God in nature and in events and yet, to see that Truth embodied in another human being is an enlightening example of our own latent capacity. Let us never underestimate the value or importance of a teacher and the importance of selecting a genuine teacher. Your own aspiration, your own inner cry, your own inner growth, if taken sincerely, will provide you with the necessary teacher. This concept may be difficult to believe, but if we truly feel and see interconnectedness, the web of life, it begins to make perfect sense. As our aspiration and inspiration unfold and grow, those things which are necessary to that continued growth will become available to us.

The majority of religious teachings declare that every human being has the birthright of a conscious oneness and integral immersion in God. For this immense journey the aid of a spiritual teacher and guide, preferably living, is of incalculable benefit.

God exists within all of us, and we will all one day realize God. A spiritual teacher is one who has found that truth and offers advice to others seeking God. It is as if you ventured into the forest and eventually came upon a beautiful clearing. After enjoying the peace and quietude of that clearing, you return to town. Your immediate reaction is to share the place you have found with others. This offering arises spontaneously from your heart, from a sense of oneness with others and the desire to share the beauty you have found with others.

As you bring your friends back to that clearing, the action is done unconditionally, if it is done with love. You do not bring them there to profit from their coming. Your reward is their joy. The same applies to a genuine spiritual teacher. Once a teacher has found Truth, they too offer it selflessly to humanity.

The great teachers say to humanity, "Look what I have discovered within myself. This Immortality, this Heaven, exists in you as well. It is not my sole possession: it is the highest aspect of us all." Just as one masters calculus, reading or writing, so also, to some is revealed the infinity of existence and the immortality of consciousness. These fortunate seekers offer their pearls of wisdom to those who have a sincere yearning to learn from them. To interact with a man or woman who has scaled the heights of humankind's potential is indeed a supreme joy.

There are those seekers who proclaim, "I can find the Truth myself. I don't need the help of another." These people unmistakably utter the truth. In the end everyone must scale that summit by his or her own volition. Yet who, upon realizing the severity and difficulty of the journey, would turn down the help or advice of another? It does not diminish one's own achievement to enlist the help of others. It is wisdom and humility that admits to the immensity of the journey and the benefit a teacher can offer.

As we wait on the banks of a river to cross to the other side, many boatmen are prepared to ply us from one shore to the other in various boats. These are the teachers of spirituality offering a path to those who seek the shore of self-realization. One can jump into the river foregoing a boat and begin swimming to the other side, but whether that is the wisest thing to do is an important question to ask ourselves before we jump into the river.

If we observe the river closely, we will see that it finds it source in the snow-capped mountains. We then realise the river will be cold. If we watch the speed of the river, we come to know the river rages. Once we have decided that we wish to cross that river, we must be careful. We must assess closely our goals and abilities and seek the best way across.

If we decide to enlist the help of a spiritual teacher in our life-journey, we must walk from boatman to boatman and ask those questions which are most important to us and listen carefully to each answer. We must read a teacher's books and study his philosophy and find if his understanding of the river resonates with ours. We must feel a confidence in the boatman and his boat.

Beyond philosophy, we must look within the boat and see if the boat is strong and seaworthy, and we must look at the other passengers in that boat, students of that teacher, and ask ourselves if they look well, if they look healthy and happy under the guidance of this boatman. How do they appear after a few days, months, years journeying in this boat?

Once we have found a boat, a path that we feel comfortable with, we must get into the boat and watch, listen, and feel with all our awareness what is going on around us. A boatman may talk about their wonderful boat and describe a great journey, yet we may step in only to find water and leaks within the boat. So, mere talk and ideas are not enough. We must see and feel the strength of the boat for ourselves. A true boatman has sailed from shore to shore many times.

Once there is a confidence, a connection between the boatman and passenger, between the student and teacher, one must listen wholeheartedly and sincerely to the requests and suggestions of the teacher. Life is truly a raging river with many unforeseen dangers, known to the boatman due to his vast experience of the river. One can always ask to be taken back to the shore from which one came and the boatman, although assuredly saddened at the loss of a passenger, will always allow the passenger to return.

The genuine teachers will declare that they will wait eternally and one day take that same passenger across the river safely.

The journey we undertake with the aid of a spiritual teacher, is a journey into our consciousness, into our own hearts and souls. The journey includes creating calm, peaceful feelings within our bodies, minds, emotions, and hearts; developing spiritual qualities, such as simplicity, sincerity, purity; and cultivating outer qualities, such as strength of body, determination and wisdom. It is a journey into our own psyches, facing our fears, understanding our dreams and slowly and patiently integrating our understanding, our view, our mind with the ultimate Truth which we seek.

The grain of sand does not become a pearl in the blink of an eye or by the mere wish to become a pearl. The process takes time. The journey from our small ego to the Infinite, the journey from our aloneness and separateness to our true connectedness and oneness with creation is a vast journey, a journey we cannot expect to take overnight.

Within our everyday life, within our sorrows, struggles, hopes and dreams, exists our perfection. Taking the help, advice and wisdom of others during our journey is not a sign of weakness or inability, but rather a sign of intelligence and wisdom. Finding one's true spiritual teacher is a great joy that does not come without effort. In our spiritual search we must dive deep into our hearts and souls and find, with all the sincerity at our command, what it is we are seeking. Once we know our goal, and are wholeheartedly committed to that goal, a teacher will definitely appear to help us.

All of existence is more interrelated and connected than we can ever imagine with our five senses. Each sense–sight, taste, touch, smell, hearing–separates us from our world, creates a separateness, an objectivity that defines "I" and "that". There does exist a wholeness, an interrelatedness, a web of consciousness, that connects all our thoughts, intentions and actions. When we are focused on our goal, we will find the correct teacher to help us towards that goal.

Once we have found a teacher who inspires us towards our goal, we begin a journey, a friendship, an interaction which is unique and fulfilling.

It is our sincerity and purity that will protect us from false teachers. All too often, in our haste or desire for the seemingly easiest method, we mistake a false teacher for a true teacher. The inner journey is long, requires perseverance and strength, yet, the goal is attainable, not by hook or by crook, but by our own determination and intensity.

The ancients texts of Indian spiritual philosophy set forth the following six stipulations which make clear a genuine spiritual teacher:

(1) The spiritual teacher must be unselfish, holy and have no desire for name, fame and wealth;

(2) The spiritual teacher must have access to soul-consciousness and be able to offer that consciousness to others. This energy which the teacher offers must be beneficial not only to the individual receiving it but to the entire world;

(3) The spiritual teacher's teachings must not contradict reason;

(4) The truths spoken of by a spiritual teacher must be accessible to all regardless of gender, caste and creed;

(5) The teachings of a spiritual teacher must not contradict the testimony–both written and spoken–of other genuine teachers;

(6) And finally, a genuine spiritual teacher knows that liberation cannot be purshased with worldly wealth. Hence, no one who claims to be able to sell spiritual enlightenment is a genuine teacher.

True teachers delight in the spiritual journey; not for wealth, name or fame, but because they know the joy and marvel of Illumination. That joy, that wonderment will sparkle in their eyes, words and deeds. They delight in showing that reality to others.

The joy, delight and intensity shining through the words, writings, actions and smile of a true spiritual teacher will be undeniable. That truth, that delight you will recognize as nothing other than your own depth, your own delight. As your teacher speaks of the goal, of the distant shore, you will know that truth to be your own: a place you know in your heart. It is then that the truth, the way, and the guide will join together with the traveler to establish a oneness and communion transcending the realm of ordinary, egotistical consciousness.

EXERCISE 10

There is an ancient saying, "When the student is ready, the teacher appears." If you do not have a spiritual teacher it is your own inner need and longing that will bring one to you. Reread the criteria for a genuine teacher on page 113. Each time you meditate offer a soulful prayer that such a teacher will come into your life.

Section III

Meditation & Daily Living

PRANA

I am taking delight in the life-breath
Flowing through my human frame,
A breath of the Infinite's Wind
Coursing through my earthen veins.

Previously I knew myself only as flesh and blood
But now, by some unknown touch,
I have come to behold and feel and intuit
A fire blazing within me
Emerging from the limitless oceans of space.

Prana, this life force, enters and sustains
My very existence
With every feeble, mortal breath I take.

Breathing in delight
I become delight and am suddenly dissolving
Into the limitless oceans of space.

16

Goals

You want to learn to meditate for a reason. It may be that you wish to relieve stress, develop certain qualities, change your attitudes, quiet your mind, develop intuition, find God and Truth or any number of other goals. The key realization is that you do have a goal. Human beings function most effectively and purposefully when they are pointed towards a goal. Take a moment and identify your primary reason for wanting to learn meditation. Remember–all reasons are equally valid and you need to give immense importance to your goal.

Be proud of your goal, regardless of the goals you think others have. Keep yourself focused on your practice, why you have begun meditation. Often people wish to learn meditation in order to relieve emotional and physical stress; or possibly, we see qualities in nature or other people which we find lacking in ourselves, and at some point we come to realise that the most effective way to cultivate these qualities in ourselves is to find a way into our own minds and hearts, a way to understand and affect our own inner workings. Meditation is a way, a very effective way. You may see and feel qualities and emotions within yourself which you would rather not have: anxiety, jealously, self-doubt and insecurity are some examples. We can, through meditation, reach for goals wherein we cultivate self-confidence, goodwill, compassion, peace and love in our minds, hearts and actions. We thereby bring these energies and feelings into the earth consciousness, making them more available to others. Once you have achieved a feeling of oneness and unity with all of existence, others will observe you and realise that if you can have such an experience then it ought to be possible for them as well. By making something–a feeling or idea–a reality you bring it closer to others.

Perhaps we are seeking answers to deep questions about our lives: who are we, where have we come from, where are we going, what is the purpose of our life? These questions can be looked at, contemplated, and answered or achieved, through the practice of daily meditation.

A key element in meditation is the idea of self-transcendence: today's goal, once achieved, becomes tomorrow's starting point. Reality, as Einstein said, is an ever-transcending reality. Reality is not static or dormant, but ever-expanding and all-encompassing. The goal that today compels us to begin meditation may in the not-too-distant future be our certain achievement and we soon find ourselves on the way to a new goal. It is very possible that this new goal was previously beyond our imaginings yet, as we journey, the unknown becomes knowable. Each time you meditate, reach for your goals wholeheartedly, with all the sincerity you can command.

When setting goals, we must learn to be honest with ourselves. Idealism is often a hindrance in that we can become overly idealistic, and, instead of dealing with what we actually are, we begin to set unrealistic goals, which, sooner or later, we realise we can never attain. This realisation will most likely cause us to lose our aspiration and motivation. Look at yourself and your situation and try to set realistic goals which are a challenge, yet within your reach. The longest journey begins with the first step. So too, our spiritual journey begins with what we can see, what we can feel, or what we can imagine. Let that be our starting point, let that be our goal. Each goal once achieved brings with it tremendous satisfaction and becomes the starting point for tomorrow's journey.

EXERCISE 11

Begin by choosing a quality you would like to cultivate in your life. It can be sincerity, simplicity, peace, love, compassion, purity, calmness or any other positive attribute. Do 3–5 minutes of relaxation-focusing exercises. Then, once you are calm and focused, concentrate on that quality. For seven inhalations silently repeat the name of the quality as you inhale. On the exhalation allow your body to relax.

Next, with each inhalation feel the essence of the quality entering into your physical body. Slowly but steadily, allow the feeling and quality to permeate your consciousness. Continue this for 5–10 minutes. Try to stay aware of that feeling, that quality, even after ending your meditation.

17

Exercise

Exercise can, if we wish to utilize it as such, play a central role in our spiritual growth. Regular exercise strengthens the body and nervous system. The body is our substance and form while on earth. By staying healthy and vigorous we are offering gratitude for the gift we have been given.

Exercise requires concentration. This concentration will help us in our meditation practice. While exercising, our mind is able to return its attention and awareness to very simple activities, such as following our breathing, becoming aware of physical movement, following a ball and various rules of a game.

A friend of mine, a successful businessman, plays handball three or four times a week in order to relax from the stress of daily business. The difference in his mental framework before and after the handball is dramatic. Dealing with business, money, problems and emergencies all day can be very stressful and can take away the mind's poise and calm. But an hour of focusing on a handball, of sweating, of focusing on breathing, or of exercising the body can rejuvenate the body, mind and spirit.

A regular exercise program need be nothing more than a daily walk, or it can be a program including running, biking, tennis, swimming, aerobics, yoga, weightlifting and many other activities. The essential factor is that we are able to focus and relax our mind in our exercise, in the simplicity of motion and action.

A healthy body facilitates the meditative process. If we are healthy, we will be able to sit quietly, allowing our body to relax. We will not be subject to various aches and pains while we sit and meditate. Often it is easier to meditate, to try to quiet and calm the mind after exercise. The transformation of our consciousness that takes place through meditation, the inpouring of light and delight from God into our lives, requires a strong, receptive vessel–our bodies.

To utilise sports and exercise as a means of spiritual growth shifts our perspective in competitive environments from the ego-based desire for victory to the self-transcending desire for the transformation of our nature through the intensity generated in our being through competition. Rather than trying to win the race to be "the best and fastest" we can use the competition to run our very best in order to find our highest capacity and strength and then work to transcend those apparent limits.

Finally, exercise is a grounding experience and gives us the opportunity to bring the energy and awareness from our meditation and anchor it firmly in our body. We must balance spirit and matter, mind and body if we are to not only find Truth, but root that Truth firmly in our earthly soil.

If we can exercise while feeling the joy, peace and focus of our meditation experiences then our activity will be inspired and motivated by spirit. We then become the true embodiment of spirit existing in and through matter. Spirit is expressed through the meditative feeling; matter is our body. We, through our very lives, are the instruments bringing spirit to matter. Exercise can be the vehicle to help us achieve this integration.

18

Diet

Our physical body seems to require food to exist. The food we eat becomes the building blocks for our physical system. This principle applies not only to the physical properties of the food we consume but also to the consciousness with which it is prepared. Our body and brain are the conduit through which our mind and senses function. Our mind is therefore interactive with the physical and psychic aspects of the food we consume. Food is God–*Annam Brahma*– it sustains our existence.

The great spiritual teacher Ramana Maharshi, when asked what was the most important form of spiritual practice in addition to practice of self-inquiry–asking the question, "Who am I?"–responded that it is a *sattvic* diet. *Sattvic* in Sanskrit means peaceful. A *sattvic* diet is a diet of mild, vegetarian foods procured by peaceful means. It is therefore suggested that if you wish to be peaceful you eat foods that do not adversely disrupt your consciousness. Such foods would include meat and fish due to the aggressive or animal consciousness they embody. The consciousness of the animal is embodied in its flesh which we then take in as food. It is helpful for the practice of meditation not to absorb lower states of consciousness in this way.

Returning to the story about Ramana Maharshi given at the beginning of this chapter–please realize that meditation is infinitely more important than diet when striving for peace of mind and heart. Many great spiritual teachers have eaten meat and fish.

Social factors, geography, and occassionally health factors may stand in the way of a vegetarian diet. I recommend a vegetarian diet when possible so that when seeking deep, lasting peace you have as many factors functioning on your behalf as possible.

The use of drugs, alcohol and tobacco is also detrimental to the calmness and health of our body, nerves and mind. These qualities are quite necessary in meditation. By eating well we energize and bring health to our body. We make ourselves fit and capable so that we can realize our highest potential. It is far easier to meditate when we are healthy and can sit for long periods without distraction. Stomach aches, head aches, digestive problems, and weak muscles are just a few of the results of not taking proper care of our health. We all have a physical body. Genetics has played its role. Two things we can actually do to change and improve our body are diet and exercise.

The consciousness of the cook preparing the food has a strong effect on the energy passed along to those eating the food. This is why a "home cooked meal," prepared with love and concern, feels so healthy and rejuvenating.

It is not the purpose of this book to take an in-depth look at nutrition and the effects of eating habits upon our bodies and consciousness. These topics are worthy of entire books and, in fact, many fine books have been written on these and related topics. I strongly suggest reading and researching this topic as it affects not only your health but the health of our children, planet and future generations.

Finally, over the years I have felt it is quite benefical to offer a moment of silent gratitude to God for the blessings of the food I have been given. Food sustains and nourishes us. By offering our thanks we sanctify our meal by acknowledging the Creator sustaining the creation.

19

Sleep

Sleep is the body's form of meditation. For most people there is nothing as relaxing or invigorating as a good night's sleep. Two essential elements of sleep which apply to meditation are the stillness and calmness of the body and the forgetting of self.

Many spiritual teachers have said that during an entire night of sleep, the body achieves a level of deep sleep for perhaps five minutes. It is during this deep sleep, that five or ten minutes, that the soul is again able to infuse the body and the entire consciousness with the eternal light, the infinite light, the soul's light. That is why, when we wake up in the morning, when we first open our eyes, we have hope, we have joy, we have happiness.

A moment after waking we allow thoughts, worries, problems, fears, and doubts into our mind and that joy, that happiness is soon lost from our awareness. The undeniable fact is that the happiness is there; we simply become distracted. A healthful, deep sleep is necessary for the body; the physical being needs to relax and rejuvenate. Yet sleep, as with so many things, can become a form of indulgence, a form of escape from conscious living. Sleeping ten or twelve hours a day is an escape. The body, a normal, healthy body, can surely get by with seven or eight hours of sleep. As we become more conscious, more alive, the desire for sleep will diminish. Our body, our system, will be able to get the healthful rest that it needs and we will be inspired and excited to wake up each morning and enjoy conscious existence.

During a lifespan of ninety years, approximately thirty years would be spent sleeping. One third of our life is spent in an unconscious state. As we become more conscious, the desire to be awake, alive, and a conscious member of society, of existence, begins to develop within our being. As we learn to calm our mind, to deal with life's situations calmly and peacefully, we will find that less time needs to be spent going to and coming from deep sleep.

It is said that one of the primary reasons for sleep is to resolve situations that we have not dealt with but have rather pushed into our subconscious. It is during sleep and dreams that these issues are confronted. Through meditation we strengthen our consciousness to the point where we no longer shy away from facing difficult situations. We learn to concentrate with such power that we resolve issues and do not need to deal with issues subconsciously. Thus, there is less need for sleep.

If the mind is calm and peaceful when we go to sleep, our sleep will be deeper, more restful, more purposeful, and more profound. If we desire, if we sincerely wish to be awake, to be alive, to be conscious more of the time, that very desire will diminish our need for sleep.

EXERCISE 12

Try to meditate for 3–5 minutes before going to sleep at night. Sit up in bed or at your meditation spot and focus on breathing in peace and calm and feeling your body relax as you exhale. Feel tranquil light and energy surrounding your body. Allow that feeling to guide you to sleep.

20

Sexual Energy

The goal of the spiritual life is conscious unity with the soul, which is part and parcel of God. The soul is eternal and infinite. The soul breathes life into nature. The soul is undifferentiated existence. It is beyond duality.

In order to consciously identify with the soul we must silence all thought, attain absolute purity and transcend nature and duality.

To attain the soul we must, at some point, let go of all thought–including sexual thoughts–in order to experience the ever-transcending purity of the soul. Thought is power and liberation requires all the power we can muster.

One of the most innate and powerful urges in nature and in human beings, is the urge to procreate. Our society has amplified this primal need to all-encompassing proportions. The regular practice of meditation will help us to truly understand the needs of our nature. The quest for spiritual experience and realization requires tremendous energy and concentration. We will discover a storehouse of energy within ourselves once we can learn to focus as much of our energy as possible towards an awareness of God.

To achieve anything requires energy. All of life is motion. To harness and direct our life energy, our motion of existence, and move our lives in a given direction requires will and effort. The more challenging and far-reaching our goals, the greater the energy and motion which are needed. At the same time, the greater the energy, the greater our will and determination must be.

The supreme goal of life is a conscious unity with God. Nothing in life is as difficult, or as rewarding, as the pursuit of this goal. In order to achieve this pinnacle-awareness, every aspect of our existence–physical, emotional and mental–must be directed towards this pursuit. The more complete our determination and intensity the sooner we will reach our goal.

Turning one's life and thoughts towards God and the eternal vastness is a supreme release. The ecstasy expressed by those who have become one with the underlying reality of existence is deeply compelling to anyone who has ever imagined this pursuit.

Sri Chinmoy, in his book on *Kundhalini Yoga*, describes such an experience:

> *"...one enjoys infinite Bliss and becomes inseparably one with the ever-transcending Beyond. One comes to know that he is birthless and deathless. He is always dealing with Infinity, Eternity and Immortality. These are not vague terms for him; they are all reality."*

Life is, in many respects, a battle with time. For the joy of conscious existence we pay the price of mortality. Death is moving ever closer, and, as we know all too well, will one day envelope our existence. Yet the existence of time and death provide us with an impetus for action. Let each of us rise to the challenge and strive towards our goals in the immediacy of today with as much intensity as possible. And now, finally, we have arrived undeniably at the heart of the matter: "with as much intensity as possible." How much intensity can we put towards our meditation, our perfection, our inner discovery, our God-ward march? How much time will we put towards the ultimate goal of life and how much towards name, fame, the pursuit of wealth, comfort and pleasure? Surely we all have the desire to pursue pleasure and to seek satisfaction through the senses. The challenge then, which all sincere seekers face, is to devote each and every life-breath towards our ultimate goal–God.

The question now becomes: How do I transform my desire for sexual gratification to a desire for God? The answer is: slowly, patiently and persistently. The transformation of human nature does not happen overnight, it is a gradual, steady process. How does one transform one's innate, primal desires? By focusing more and more on aspects of God with which one feels an affinity. God is knowledge–read; God is beauty–create; God is delight–smile; God is humanity–help others; God is your body–get healthy. In other words, focus your attention as much as possible towards your ultimate goal.

The incorrect way to transform sexual energy is through suppression. The very nature of suppression embodies pressure. This pressure–"pent-up emotion"–will eventually explode, and when it does, damage is sure to occur.

Indulgence is not the answer either. Indulgence only leads to frustration for the simple reason that we can never truly satisfy ourselves through the senses.

The answer is transformation. The transformation of our human nature into a divine, or spiritual, nature is the very purpose of life. Our growing awareness of God is also God's descent into us. To prepare ourselves to receive God is the most challenging, yet most fulfilling undertaking a human being can attempt. To allow the dust and clay of our mortal frame to be filled with the light and delight of Eternity is a great and noble undertaking. One aspect of this undertaking is the transformation of our emotional, earth-bound nature, which includes our sexual energy.

My experience has shown me that the safest and most effective means to bring about this transformation are regular meditation, physical fitness and creativity. Sports and creative pursuits allow for a sense of joy, freedom, abandonment and release. As we create we bring new life into existence; as we run, walk, jump and play we lose our fear and worry and merge into the delight of a child's heart.

Another aspect of transformation involves infusing our human activities with an awareness of God. One of the delights of this practice is the ability to see and feel God in everyone and everything. The poet-philosopher Sri Aurobindo expresses this realization beautifully:

"See yonder old man who passes near you crouching and bent, with his stick. Do you realize that it is God who is passing? There a child runs laughing in the sunlight. Can you hear Him in that laughter?"

If we can learn to see and feel God in every aspect of earth-life then every activity becomes a sacred event infused with the delight of the Infinite in the finite. From this awareness we find God in all, in pain and pleasure, birth and death, victory and defeat.

The transformation of life necessitates an acceptance of life. Our acceptance and delight of living can only rest upon one thought and realization–all is God.

21

Intensity

No journey is as difficult or as satisfying as the journey of self-discovery. To allow oneself to merge with, to surrender to, to be inundated with the Divine is an adventure in consciousness that requires an utmost intensity and aspiration.

Sri Ramakrishna, a spiritual teacher who lived in India in the middle of the 19th century, used to tell a wonderful story conveying the level of intensity necessary for the attainment of God:

"A student once asked a spiritual master what kind of intensity was necessary to reach

the ultimate goal. The teacher invited his student to take a walk. Eventually, they ended up on the banks of a river. The teacher went into the river, stood in the water, and invited the student to join him. The teacher then put the student's head under water holding it firmly. Eventually, the student began to run out of air and tried to lift his head out of the water, at which point the master resisted. Finally, the student, with all his strength, overpowered the teacher's hold and emerged gasping for air. The teacher smiled and said, 'When you have that same intensity for God and Truth, you will realize the ultimate goal.'"

Spiritual growth and the expansion of consciousness into an awareness of God is a vast undertaking. It is far more difficult than the acquisition and memorization of intellectual knowledge, more difficult than ethical and moral reasoning and more difficult than scientific understanding. The reason for this is that the spiritual journey requires not merely the acquisition, memorization and pondering of new thoughts, but a control and mastery of the thought process. Furthermore, one must learn to step away from and entirely observe the thought process. The vantage point from which this observation takes place is the realm beyond thought, the reality and formation of which is the next step in the evolution of human consciousness. To step above the whirlpool of thoughts is to enter the realm of the spiritual heart wherein the prevailing power is the love and compassion of unity and oneness and not the division-reality and ego force of the mind and vital consciousness.

This process requires all of the best qualities available to you: sincerity, simplicity, purity, determination, truthfulness, perseverance, strength and so many other aspects of God immersed in human form.

The evolution of consciousness is the supreme achievement of life. The thought or desire for God and Truth soon gives birth to inspiration–the source of action. When we begin to consciously seek God with all the fervor available to us then we are entering the realm of aspiration. Aspiration blossoms into realization.

Maintain a bright, joyful intensity in your practice, yet steer clear of expectation. When we begin to expect certain meditative experiences then we are beginning to limit the shape and form that God's living breath can take for us and manifest in and through us.

Intensity, determination and a cheerful surrender to God's Will is the sure way to sail straight into God's Heart.

22

Keep Going

Continued progress in meditation and spirituality requires determination and perseverance. Many great writers, when asked to what they would attribute their success, have alluded to the simple discipline of sitting down and writing 1000 words a day, every day. Meditation demands the same.

Each of us, regardless of our potential, will achieve little without discipline and sincere effort. We must unearth a sense of peace, fun, joy and humor in our meditation practice and in our lives. Taking ourselves or our practice too seriously is a mistake. There is a difference between overconcern and intensity. The ability to laugh at oneself, to not take oneself too seriously is essential. Meditation, true meditation, is constantly new, fresh and alive. We must learn to enjoy experiencing new things, undertaking new tasks and enjoying new experiences. Each day, each moment, each meditation ought to embody newness and freshness.

In order to inspire ourselves for meditation, it is a good idea to set realistic goals which are within our reach, yet require a solid effort. Developing certain qualities such as simplicity, sincerity and purity are wonderful goals. We can bring these qualities into our lives and focus on these feelings. In addition to inner goals, outer goals of health and a positive direction for our lives are actualized by the meditation process.

It is important to give oneself credit when credit is due. Mark your achievements and successes; they are significant. Self-motivation is one of the primary keys to success. Keep yourself inspired and motivated yet all the time maintain a balance between work and play, between intensity and the ability to observe yourself with objectivity; allow yourself both smiles and tears.

Through meditation we learn to understand ourselves, to see what gives us satisfaction, to see what inspires us. We begin to observe and understand those experiences and situations which diminish our aspiration and sense of self-worth. Always focus on your successes, and view defeat as a necessary step in the learning process.

Meditation creates a clarity through which we can observe ourselves and our environment. By applying that clarity to all we say and do, we will learn and grow from all of our life experiences. This growth will immediately create the inspiration for our continued practice. Each step we take brings our goal that much closer.

23

Starting a Meditation Group

"The light that shines above the heavens and above this world, the light that shines in the highest world, beyond which there are no others–that is the light that shines in the hearts of men."

- Chandogya Upanishad
(ancient scripture of India)

One of the greatest joys of living is to bring the light, so beautifully described in the above passage, into our own lives and into the lives of others. We can bring this light forward from the depths of our spirit by setting aside time each day for meditation, self-reflection and conscious relaxation. Through these and other related activities we bring peace, balance, insight and harmony into our bodies, minds, emotions and spirit.

In addition to daily, individual meditation, it is also an enriching experience to join together with others in a group setting for a collective meditation. To enjoy the benefits of group meditation you can either find a meditation group with which you feel comfortable, or, as this chapter will help you to do, you can form and organize your own meditation group.

Since 1979 I have meditated on a regular basis and, as part of my practice, participated in a group meditation at least once a week. This meditation lasts for one hour and is the spiritual highlight of my week. After the meditation we enjoy a light meal or snack and some conversation. There are not many people on earth who meditate, therefore I value the opportunity to spend time with those who do.

If you do not currently attend a regular group meditation, or have not found a group with which you are comfortable, you can start your own meditation group. The following are some ideas and guidelines to help you start a meditation group.

Philosophy

I suggest shaping your practice around the basic philosophy put forward in the quote at the beginning of this chapter. The practice of meditation helps us awaken to the light and soul which unifies all of existence. The weekly group meditation is a gathering of individuals aspiring to intensify their awareness of their own divinity and greater potential. It is also an offering of peace to the earth consciousness. We see all around us the powers and forces of anger, frustration, destruction and selfishness. To bring into this world of ours qualities such as peace, calmness and gratitude is indeed a significant achievement. This is the power of, and philosophy behind, true meditation.

I suggest finding readings from the world's religious and spiritual scriptures which draw out this theme and having 10 to 15 minutes of reading aloud during each group meditation.

Group Size

I would suggest you aspire toward a group size of 12 people or more. The force of 12 people praying or meditating together is cited in ancient scripture as the number necessary to invoke God's presence on earth. Of course, you will most likely begin with a smaller number, yet the sincerity and purity of your practice will draw other sincere seekers. Meditation helps us to develop inner peace and calm–these lead to abiding happiness, which everyone desires. When others see these qualities in you they will be drawn to the practice of meditation. Through these types of interactions your group will grow.

Location

Choose a location where the group can meet for two hours once each week, on the same night. It would be ideal if the meditation area–a living room or extra room in a house or apartment–could be used solely for meditation. This will allow for a subtle atmosphere of peace and tranquility to grow in that area.

Room Set-up

Our consciousness is affected by that which our senses perceive. We want to create a meditation room which will bring soothing qualities to our senses. To accomplish this, I recommend light, bright colors such as white, gold and blue; a well-lit room; incense and at one end of the room a shrine or altar toward which those present will face. On this shrine I suggest flowers and a candle or two. These will serve to purify and beautify the room and create objects for visual focusing. I also suggest that women sit on the left side of the room, men on the right. This type of seating aligns the group energy to be in balance with the universal energy of duality in oneness. In the human body the left nostril brings feminine, moon energy into the system while the right nostril connects to the masculine, sun energy. This type of seating is a recognition of the polarities of creation yet also sings the song of oneness. This seating also allows each individual freedom from immediate distractions.

Structure of the Meditation Session

Begin the one-hour session with five minutes of chanting the *mantra*, seed sound, Aum; then a ten-minute reading; then 35 minutes of either silent meditation or meditation with soft background music; then another five-minute reading and finally, to conclude, five minutes of chanting the *mantra* Yam.

Each chant ought to last ten seconds, seven seconds creating the sound and three for the inhalation. To begin, play a middle F on the piano, keyboard or other instrument and have everyone hum and attune to that note; then do all the chanting on that note. The final "m" sound of each *mantra* will account for two-thirds of the chant.

If you decide to play music during the meditation, be sure it was created specifically for meditation by people who do meditation. For the reading section I suggest either individual silent readings or text that reflects the philosophy stated earlier. I suggest readings from the *Gospels*, the *Koran*, *Old Testament*, the *Dhamapada*, the *Vedas*, the *Tao Te Ching*, *Bhagavad-Gita* and *Upanishads*.

The *mantra* Aum is the universal seed sound and connects one with all of life. Yam is the *mantra* to awaken the heart center, the center of love, compassion and oneness in each individual.

The Day and Hour for Meditation

I recommend beginning the meditation at 7:30 pm and holding the session in the middle of the week–Tuesday, Wednesday or Thursday. This will give everyone a mid-week "pick-me-up" to look forward to. Sunday evening is also a pleasant time for group meditation.

Group Effort

Each week the group can choose a quality or attribute which everyone can try to cultivate during the meditation. This quality or theme can be the focus of the selected readings. Attributes can include simplicity, sincerity, purity, compassion, acceptance, understanding, love, unity and gratitude.

Leadership

The soul and spirit of each seeker guides that individual's inner awakening. In order to maintain the structure of the group, individuals will need to accept various responsibilities, i.e. location, lighting, food, selection of readings, leading the chanting, etc. Keeping these two types of leadership, inner and outer, clearly defined will assure the success of the group. The readings from various scriptures help each individual's mind to invoke and accept the light of their soul or psychic being.

Afterward

I suggest vegetarian snacks or a light meal following the meditation. This allows everyone the opportunity to assimilate their meditation experience and enjoy pleasant interaction with those fellow seekers with whom they have journeyed toward the source of existence.

I have no doubt that this weekly meditation-gathering will soon prove to be one of the highlights of your week and a great source of personal energy, strength and inspiration.

24

Conclusion

This book has been an attempt to offer you some basic, fundamental ideas concerning meditation. More importantly, you have tried the actual practice of meditation and created for yourself a meditation area. There are a few important points that run throughout the book that I wish to once again emphasize. First is the importance of the cultivation of wisdom, purity and peacefulness within your consciousness. These qualities combine to create the proper foundation which is essential for the journey of self-discovery.

It is also essential to learn to trust your own feelings and intuitions with regard to philosophies, groups, techniques and teachers you may encounter while searching for your own unique path to God. Always gage or view experiences or ideas from the vantage point of your own sincere, innate happiness. Listen to your heart–your spiritual heart–trust the subtle wisdom of your heart and soul. It is essential to follow your own thoughts and feelings. We all must learn to believe in ourselves, and our sublime, soulful wisdom.

Remember the importance of a teacher. As with all other pursuits in our lives, the aid of a teacher is a tremendous benefit. Finding your spiritual mentor is one of the greatest joys of human evolution. To see in another the qualities which we wish to find and manifest in our own lives creates inspiration, aspiration, motivation, hope, action and a constant flow of satisfaction.

Remember, we are all integrally connected. Your spiritual growth is everyone's spiritual growth. Each step you take towards oneness and unity of consciousness is a step taken for humanity. In our oneness with humanity, we come to understand the interconnectedness that exists within all beings. That knowledge, that wisdom, is indeed the supreme ecstasy and potential of life.

Finally, remember God. Open yourself daily, through your meditation, to the infinite source of pure love which permeates your very existence at this very moment.

Peace... Aum... Peace.

Suggested Readings

I have touched on a wide variety of topics in this book. Many of these topics warrant further reading and study. For this reason I have enclosed a suggested reading list. This list begins with the principal scriptures upon which the teachings of the world religions are based:

Aurobindo, Sri. *The Message of the Gita* (India: Sri Aurobindo Ashram Press, 1938).

Brown, Brian. *The Wisdom of the Chinese* (Garden City Publishing Co. Inc., New York, 1920).

The Dhammapada. Translated by Irving Babbit (New York: New Directions Publishing Corporation, 1936).

Holy Bible: From the Ancient Eastern Text. Translated by George M. Lamsa. (San Francisco: Harper, 1933).

Lao Tzu. *Tao Te Ching: The Way of Life.* Translated by Raymond B. Blackney (New York: New American Library, 1955).

Lao Tzu. *Tao Teh Ching.* Translated by Dr. John C. H. Wu (New York: St. John's University Press, 1973).

Prabhavananda, Swami. *The Song of God: Bhagavad-Gita* (New York: Signet, 1944).

Prabhavananda, Swami. *The Upanishads: Breath of the Eternal* (Hollywood; Vedanta Press, 1947).

Radhakrishnan, S. *The Bhagavadgita* (San Francisco: Harper & Row, 1948).

The Upanishads. Translated by Max Müller (New York: Dover Publications, 1962 [first published in 1879]).

In addition to these specific books there are certain authors and spiritual figurs I highly recommend who have a number of books to their credit: Sri Aurobindo, Sri Chinmoy, Loren Eisley, Ralph Waldo Emerson, the Sri Ramakrishna Mission, Ramana Maharshi, Henry David Thoreau and Swami Vivekananda.

All totaled, these authors have over 1,000 books to their credit on a wide range of spiritual topics.

On the topic of food and diet I recommend *Diet for a New America* by John Robbins. For an understanding of Hatha Yoga and the philosophy upon which it is based I suggest *Light on Yoga* by B.K.S. Iyengar.

A well written book by a knowledgeable author will lead you to countless other books and writings. Through books we are able to study the thoughts and realizations of men and women throughout history. This study and the lines of thought thereby uncovered is a very personal journey. You will, in your own sojourn, uncover writings and authors I have never read... and so it should be. By beginning your journey with one or more of the authors I have suggested you will be starting with ideas and concepts that are of the highest quality in recorded history. By beginning here you will be able to recognize and steer clear of some of the hazards of spiritual philosophy–poor translation, faulty or one-sided interpretations and finally–and the worst of all– direct manipulation of philosophy and ideas to influence the thoughts and behavior of others.

Finally, and with sincere humility, I recommend my other two writings: *Paths are Many, Truth is One* and *Strategy for Success.*